Machine Learning for Business

How to Build Artificial Intelligence through Concepts of Statistics, Algorithms, Analysis, and Data Mining

Finley Peters

ISBN: 9798633573329

Table of Contents

Introduction

Congratulations on purchasing Machine Learning for Business: Study Deep Learning through Data Science. How to build artificial intelligence through concepts of statistics, algorithms, analysis and data mining

The following chapters discuss the fundamental concepts of machine learning algorithms and the need for machine learning in solving modern business problems. The first chapter of this book provides a detailed explanation of the four different types of machine learning algorithms currently available on the market, along with the importance of machine learning. Representation, evaluation and optimization are the three core concepts of machine learning that are explained in detail. You will be introduced to the concept of "Statistical Learning", a descriptive statistic-based machine learning framework that can be categorized as supervised or unsupervised.

In Chapter 3 of this book entitled "Machine Learning Algorithms", you will learn the development and application of some of the most popular supervised machine learning algorithms, with explicit details on linear regression, logistic regression and Naïve Bayes classification algorithms. In Chapter 4, entitled "Neural Network Learning Models," it provides an overarching guide to everything you need to know for the successful development of neural network models by learning how to build data pipelines for your machine learning models and then follow specific neural network training approaches. The end-to-end process described in this chapter provides you with an overarching look at how to generate your desired machine learning model from scratch, with an emphasis on neural network models. You will also learn the different components and functions that play in the Artificial Neural Network and Perceptron (single neuron-based network) models, as well as different applications of these advanced and futuristic machine learning models to solve everyday business problems.
In the fourth chapter of this book, entitled "Learning through uniform convergence", we will discuss the overlap of machine learning in the field of statistics. One of the many borrowed statistical concepts used in the development of machine learning models is "Uniform Convergence", which allows the developer to identify the learnability of the problem based on the size of the data sample using empirical risk minimizers. You will gain in-depth knowledge of the concept of "General Setting of Learning", introduced by Vapnik in 1995 and remain at the center of the concept of machine learning development. A statistical explanation is given of the impact of "Uniform Convergence" on learnability as a requirement with finite classes, together with a discussion of potential learnability without "Uniform Convergence".

The final chapter of this book provides you with a holistic overview of several advanced data science technologies such as data mining and artificial intelligence. The most recommended lifecycle for structured data science projects is that the "Team Data Science Process" (TDSP) is explained in great detail, along with different deliverables to be generated at each stage. You also learn how data science is used by companies in their decision-making process. The power of artificial intelligence has already begun to manifest in our environment and our everyday objects. So you need to learn the difference between Business Intelligence and Data Science technology. This book is packed with real-world examples to help you understand the core concepts and names and description of multiple tools that you can further explore and selectively implement in your business to reap the benefits of these advanced technologies.

There are plenty of books on the subject on the market, thanks again for choosing this one! Every effort has been made to ensure that it contains as much useful information as possible, have fun!

Chapter 1: Introduction to machine learning

The idea of artificial intelligence technology is derived from the idea that computers can be designed to display human-like intelligence and mimic human reasoning and learning abilities, adapt to new inputs and perform tasks without human intervention. The principle of artificial intelligence includes machine learning. Machine Learning Technology (ML) refers to the principle of Artificial Intelligence Technology, which mainly focuses on the designed ability of computers to explicitly learn and train themselves, identifying information patterns to improve the underlying algorithm and making autonomous decisions without human intervention. In 1959, the term "machine learning" was coined during his tenure at IBM by the pioneering professor of gaming and artificial intelligence, Arthur Samuel.

Machine learning assumes that modern computers can be trained using targeted training datasets, which can be easily modified to create the required functionality. Machine learning is guided by a pattern recognition method where previous interactions and results are recorded and reviewed in a way that matches the current position. Because machines are required to process infinite amounts of data and new data is constantly coming in, they must be equipped to adapt to the new data without being programmed by a person, given the iterative aspect of machine learning. Machine learning has close relationships with the Statistics field, which focuses on generating predictions using advanced computer tools and technologies. The research on "mathematical optimization" offers the field of machine learning with techniques, theories and implementation areas. Machine learning is also referred to as 'predictive analysis' during implementation to address business problems. In ML, the 'target' is known as 'label', while statistics refer to it as 'dependent variable'. A 'variable' in statistics is known in ML as a 'feature'. And a "feature creation" in ML is known as "transformation" in statistics.

ML technology is also closely related to data mining and optimization. ML and data mining often use the same techniques with significant overlap. ML focuses on generating predictions based on predefined characteristics of the given training data. On the other hand, data mining involves identifying unknown features in a large data volume. Data mining uses many ML techniques, but with different objectives; similarly, machine learning also uses data mining techniques through the "uncontrolled learning algorithms" or as a preprocessing phase to improve the prediction accuracy of the model. The intersection of these two different research areas stems from the fundamental assumptions they work with. In machine learning, efficiency is generally judged by the model's ability to reproduce known knowledge, while in "knowledge discovery and information mining (KDD)" the main task is to discover new information. An "uninformed or uncontrolled" technique, evaluated in terms of known information, will easily be surpassed by other "controlled techniques". On the contrary, "guided techniques" cannot be used in a typical "KDD" task due to the lack of training data. Data optimization is another area that machine learning is closely associated with. Several learning difficulties can be formulated as minimizing certain "loss functions" on training data set. Loss functions are derived as the difference between the predictions generated by the trained model and the input data values. The distinction between the two areas stems from the objective of "generalization". Optimization algorithms are designed to reduce the loss of the training data set. The goal of machine learning is to minimize the loss of real-world input data.

Machine learning has become such a "heated" problem that its definition varies across the world of academia, business and the scientific community. Here are some of the generally accepted definitions of selected sources that are extremely well known:

• "Machine learning is based on algorithms that can learn from data without relying on rule-based programming." McKinsey.
• "Machine learning is basically the practice of using algorithms to parse data, learn from it, and then make a determination or prediction about something in the world." - Nvidia
• "The Machine Learning area tries to answer the question, how can we build computer systems that automatically improve with experience, and what are the fundamental laws that govern all learning processes? - Carnegie Mellon University
• "Machine learning is the science of making computers act without being explicitly programmed." Stanford University

Chapter 2: Types of machine learning

Machine learning under supervision

Guided machine learning is widely used in predictive big data analysis because it allows them to assess and apply the lessons learned from previous iterations and interactions to new data sets. These learning algorithms can label all their current events based on the given instructions to efficiently predict and predict future events. For example, the machine can be programmed to label the data points as "R" (Run), "N" (Negative), or "P" (Positive). The machine-learning algorithm then labels the input data as programmed and receives the correct output data. The algorithm compares its own production with the "expected or correct" output, identifies potential changes and fixes errors to make the model more accurate and smarter. By using methods such as "regression", "" prediction "," "classification" and "enhancement of ingredients" to properly train the learning algorithms, all new input data can be fed to the machine as a "target" data set to display the learning program such as desirable. This gives a flying start to the analysis and drives the learning algorithms to create a "derivative function", which can be used to generate predictions and predictions based on output values for future events. For example, financial organizations and banks rely heavily on machine learning algorithms to detect credit card fraud and predict the likelihood that a potential customer will not pay their loan on time.

Machine learning without supervision

Companies are often in a situation where data sources required to generate a labeled and categorized training data set are not available. Under these circumstances, using unsupervised machine learning is ideal. "Uncontrolled learning algorithms" are often used to describe how the machine can produce "derived attributes" to illustrate hidden patterns of an unlabeled and unclassified component in the data stack. These algorithms can explore the data so that a structure can be defined within the data mass. While unsupervised automatic learning algorithms are just as effective as supervised learning algorithms at exploring input and gaining insights, unattended algorithms are unable to identify the correct output. These algorithms can be used to define outliers for data; to tailor product suggestions; to classify text topics using techniques such as "self-organizing maps", "singular decomposition" and "k-means clustering". Customer identification, for example, customers can be segmented into groups with shared shopping attributes and targeted with similar marketing strategies and campaigns. Consequently, unsupervised learning algorithms are very common in the online marketing industry.

Semi-supervised machine learning

The semi-supervised machine learning algorithms are extremely flexible and can learn from both labeled and unlabeled or raw data. These algorithms are a "hybrid" of supervised and uncontrolled ML algorithms. Typically, the training data set consists of predominantly unlabeled data and a small portion of the labeled data. The use of analytical methods such as "prediction", "regression" and "classification" in combination with semi-controlled learning algorithms allows the computer to significantly improve its accuracy in learning and training. These algorithms are often used when the production of processed and labeled training data from the raw dataset is very resource intensive and less cost effective for the company. Companies use their systems with semi-guided learning algorithms to avoid additional personnel and equipment costs. For example, the application of "facial recognition" technology requires a huge amount of facial data across multiple input sources. Processing, classifying, and labeling raw data from sources, including Internet cameras, requires a lot of resources and thousands of hours to use as a training data set.

Strengthening machine learning

The 'machine learning amplification algorithm' learns from its environment and is much more unique than any machine learning algorithms discussed earlier. Such algorithms perform activities and carefully record the results of each action, either as an error for a failed outcome or as a reward for excellent results. The two main features that distinguish the reinforcement learning algorithm are the "trial and error" analysis technique and the "delayed reward" feedback loop. The computer continuously analyzes input data using various calculations and sends a gain signal for any correct or intended output to ultimately optimize the final results. The algorithm creates an easy action and rewards feedback loop for assessing, recording and learning what activity has been efficient in the sense that it resulted in the correct or intended output in a shorter time. By using such algorithms, the system can automatically determine optimal behavior and maximize its effectiveness in a specific context. That is why the reinforcing machine learning algorithms are used intensively in the disciplines of gaming, robotics and navigation systems.

Importance of machine learning

The seemingly unstoppable interest in ML stems from the same variables that "data mining" and "Bayesian analysis" have done more than ever before. The underlying factors contributing to this popularity are increasing amounts and varieties of data, cheaper and more effective computational processing, and cheap data storage. To get an idea of how important machine learning is in our daily lives, it's easier to pinpoint which part of our advanced way of life hasn't been affected. Every aspect of human life is influenced by the "smart machines" that are designed to expand human capabilities and improve efficiency. Artificial intelligence and machine learning technology is the central premise of the "fourth industrial revolution" that may cast doubt on our "human" thoughts.

All these factors imply that models that can analyze larger, more complicated data while delivering highly accurate results in a short time can be produced quickly and automatically on a much larger scale. Businesses can easily identify potential growth opportunities or avoid unknown dangers by constructing desired machine learning models that meet their business requirements. Data runs through the veins of every company. Data-driven strategies are increasingly distinguishing between winning or losing the competition. Machine learning offers the magic of unlocking the importance of business and customer data to lead to actionable measures and decisions that can skyrocket a company's business and market share.

Machine learning has shown in recent years that many different tasks can be automated that were once considered human-only activities, such as image recognition, word processing and gaming. In 2014, Machine Learning and AI professionals thought the board game "Go" would take at least ten years for the machine to defeat its biggest player in the world. But they turned out to be mistaken by "Google's DeepMind", which showed that machines can learn which movements to take into account, even in such a complicated game as "Go". In the world of gaming, machines have seen many more innovations, such as "Dota Bot" from the "OpenAI" team. Machine learning undoubtedly has enormous economic and social consequences for our daily lives. A full range of work activities and the entire industrial spectrum could potentially be automated and the labor market will be transformed forever.

> "Machine learning is a data analysis method that automates the building of analytical models. It is a branch of artificial intelligence based on the idea that systems can learn from data, identify patterns and make decisions with minimal human intervention."
>
> - SAS

Automation of repetitive learning and information disclosure

Unlike robot automation powered by hardware that only automates manual tasks, machine learning continuously and reliably enables the execution of large quantities, large volumes and computer-oriented tasks. Machine learning algorithms of artificial intelligence help adapt to the changing landscape by enabling a machine or system to learn, learn and reduce past errors. Machine learning algorithm works as a classifier or forecasting tool to develop unique skills and define data pattern and structure. For example, a machine learning algorithm has created a model that teaches itself chess and even creates product suggestions based on consumer activity and behavioral data. This model is so effective because it can easily adapt to any new data set. Machine learning allows deeper and broader datasets to be assessed using neural networks that contain several hidden layers. Just a few years ago, a fraud detection scheme with numerous hidden layers would be considered an imagination. A whole new world is upon us with the advent of big data and unimaginable computing possibilities. The data on the machines is like the gas on the vehicle, adding more data leads to faster and more accurate results. Deep learning models thrive on a wealth of data because they directly benefit from the information. The machine learning algorithms have led to incredible accuracy through the "deep neural networks". Increased accuracy is achieved through deep learning, for example through the regular and extensive use of smart technology such as "Amazon Alexa" and "Google Search". These 'deep neural networks' also stimulate our healthcare. Technologies such as image classification and object recognition can now detect cancer with the same precision as a highly qualified radiologist on MRIs.

Thanks to artificial intelligence, the use of big data analysis in combination with the machine learning algorithm can be improved and improved. Data has evolved like their currency and can easily become "intellectual property" when algorithms are self-learning. The raw information is similar to that of a gold mine: the more and more you dig, the more you can dig or extract "gold" or meaningful insights. Using machine learning algorithms for the data enables faster discovery of the right solutions and can make these solutions more useful. Keep in mind that the best data will always be the winner, even if everyone uses similar techniques.

'People can usually make one or two good models a week; machine learning can create thousands of models per week. "
- Thomas Davenport, The Wall Street Journal

Core concepts of machine learning

Today there are different types of ML, but the term ML is mainly based on three components: "representation", "evaluation" and "optimization". Here are some of the standard concepts that apply to all of them:

Representation

Machine learning models cannot directly hear, see or feel input samples. Data representation is therefore necessary to provide the model with a useful point of view in the main data attributes. The choice of significant attributes that best represent data is very essential to effectively train a machine learning model. "Representation" simply refers to "representing" data points to a computer in a language that it understands using a set of classifications. A classifier can be defined as "a model that inputs a vector of discrete and / or continuous function values and outputs a single discrete value called" class. "To learn from the data presented, a model must have the desired classifier in the training dataset or "hypothesis space" that you want the models to be trained on. The data functions used to represent the input are critical to the machine learning system. Any "classifier" that is outside the hypothesis space cannot Learning the model To develop a required machine learning model, data attributes are so essential that it can easily be the difference between successful and unsuccessful machine learning projects.

A training data set with several independent 'functions' that are well linked to the 'class' can make learning for the machine much easier. On the other hand, it may not be easy for the machine to learn from the classroom with complex functions. This often requires the processing of the raw data so that the desired features for the ML model can be built from it. The method of deriving functions from raw data collection is often the most time-consuming and labor-intensive part of the ML project. It is also considered to be the most creative and interesting part of the project where intuition and trial and error play as important a role as the technical requirements. The ML process is not a one-shot process for developing and executing a training data set, but an iterative process that requires analysis of the output after execution, followed by modification of the training data set. Domain specificity is another reason why the training data set takes a lot of time and effort. Training data set to produce predictions based on consumer behavior analysis for an ecommerce platform will be very different from the training data set required to create a self-driving car. Nevertheless, in the industrial sectors, the main mechanism of machine learning remains the same. No wonder there is a lot of research going on to automate the feature engineering process.

Evaluation

Essentially, in the context of ML, "evaluation" is called the method of assessing different hypotheses or models to select one model over another. An "evaluation function" is needed to distinguish between effective classifications and the vague classifications. The evaluation function is also known as the "objective", "utility" or "score" function. The machine learning algorithm has an internal evaluation function that is usually very different from the researchers' external evaluation function used to optimize the classifier. Usually the evaluation function is described as the first stage of the project before selecting the data representation tool. For example, the self-driving car machine learning model has the function of identifying nearby pedestrians at near zero, false negative and low error
positive percentage as an "evaluation function" and the pre-existing state to be "represented" using appropriate data functions.

Optimization

The process of searching the hypothesis space of the represented machine learning model to identify the highest scoring classifier and achieve better evaluation is called "optimization". For algorithms with more than one optimal classifier, selecting the optimization method is critical in determining the generated classifier and achieving a more effective learning model. There are several "out-of-the-box optimizers" on the market to launch new machine learning models before replacing them with custom designed optimizers.

Statistical learning framework

Statistical learning is a descriptive, statistics-based learning framework that can be categorized as supervised or unsupervised. "Controlled statistical learning" involves constructing a statistical model to predict or estimate output based on single or multiple inputs. On the other hand, "uncontrolled statistical learning" includes inputs, but not supervisory output, but helps in learning data relationships and structure. One way to understand statistical learning is to identify the relationship between the "predictor" (autonomous variables, attributes) and the "response" (autonomous variable), to produce a specific model that is able to " response variable (Y) "Based on" predictive factors (X) ".
"$X = f(X) + \varepsilon$ where $X = (X1, X2, ..., Xp)$", where "f" is an "unknown function" and "ε " is a "random error (reducible and irreducible)" .
Here are some basic concepts of statistical learning:

Forecast and inference

If multiple inputs "X" are easily accessible, but the output "B" production is unknown, "f" is often treated as a black box, provided it generates accurate predictions for "Y". This is called "prediction". There are circumstances in which we need to understand how

"Y" is affected when "X" changes. We want to estimate "f" in this scenario, but our goal is not just to generate predictions for "Y". In this situation, we want to establish and better understand the relationship between "Y" and "X". Now "f" is not considered a black box because we need to understand the underlying process of the system. This is called "inference." In daily life, different problems can be divided into the setting of 'predictions', the setting of 'inferences' or a 'hybrid' of the two.

Parametric and non-parametric techniques

The "parametric technique" can be defined as an evaluation of "f" by calculating the set parameters (finite summary of the data) while establishing an assumption about the functional form of "f". The mathematical equation of this technique is "f $(X) = \beta 0 + \beta 1 X1 + \beta 2 X2 + . . . + \beta p Xp$ ". The "parametric models" usually have a finite number of parameters that are independent of the size of the data set. This is also referred to as 'model-based learning'. For example, 'K-Gaussian models' are driven by parametric technique.

On the other hand, 'non-parametric technique' generates an estimate of 'f' based on the proximity of the data points, without making assumptions about the functional form of 'f'. The "non-parametric models" tend to have a varying number of parameters that have grown in proportion to the size of the data set. This is also known as 'memory-based learning'. For example, 'kernel density models' are driven by a non-parametric technique.

Predictions Accuracy and model interpretability

Some of the many methods used to learn from statistics are less adaptable and extremely restrictive. When "inference" is the goal, using easy and relatively inflexible statistical learning techniques has significant advantages. On the other hand, if the goal is to generate predictions and predictions, flexible models are preferred.

The performance of the model can be estimated based on the accuracy to predict the occurrence of an event on new input data. A more accurate model is considered a more valuable model. Interpretability of the model provides insight into the input-output relationship. An interpreted model can provide insight into the ability of independent attributes to generate predictions for the dependent attribute. The problem occurs because,

at the expense of interpretability, as the accuracy of the model improves, the complexity of the model also increases.

A more accurate model can offer a company more options, benefits, time or money. But model accuracy needs to be optimized for such a prediction. The optimization of accuracy further increases the complexity of the model by introducing additional model parameters (and means needed to adjust those parameters). A model with a relatively small number of parameters is much easier and faster to interpret. An input coefficient and an interception term are part of a linear regression model. For example, any term can be explored to assess how it contributes to output production. Switching to a logistic regression model gives more authority. In the context of the relationships underlying the potential transformation of a function to output, this must also be investigated together with the coefficients.

It is relatively easy to understand a small-sized decision tree, but a heavily loaded decision tree needs a clear perspective to understand why the event is expected to occur. In addition, the optimized combination of different models in one forecast tends to have no significant or timely interpretation. Interpretation is considered to be additional to model accuracy. For example, models designed to separate and classify "spam" emails from "non-spam" emails, as well as

models designed to evaluate the price of real estate.

Assess model accuracy

There is no one-size-fits-all or handyman technique in the field of statistics, it is impossible for a single technique to dominate the enormous variety of data sets. The most commonly used metric in the "regression" environment is the "mean square error (MSE)", which can be used to quantify the closeness of the "predicted response value" to the actual response value for the target observation. that are very close to the real responses, the MSE is calculated as small, but if the predicted and true responses vary significantly with respect to some of the observations, the MSE is calculated as large. For example, assume that we have clinical data for some patients, such as their weight, blood pressure, gender, age, history of familial illness, along with information about whether they have diabetes or not. This patient-related data set can be used to train a statistical technique for predicting diabetes risk based on clinical measures.

$$MSE = \frac{1}{n} \sum_{i=1}^{n} (y_i - \hat{f}(x_i))^2.$$

The most commonly used metric in the "classification" environment is the "confusion matrix". The main characteristic of statistical learning is that with continuous learning the model becomes more flexible and training errors are reduced, although the test error may not be reduced.

Bias and deviation

In the context of machine learning, bias is defined as 'the simplified assumptions made by a model to further simplify learning the target task'. Parametric models are designed with an inherently strong bias, making learning much faster and easier, but significantly reducing the overall flexibility of the model for a wider variety of applications. "Decision trees", "k neighbors", and "vector support machines" are categorized as low bias algorithms for machine learning models. The "high bias" ML algorithms are "linear regression", "linear discriminant analysis", and "logistic regression".
In machine learning, a variance can be defined "as the amount by which the target function estimate will be changed using a different training data set". Non-parametric models "with high flexibility tend to have a high variance score." Linear regression "," linear discriminant analysis "and" logistic regression "are low variance ML algorithms." Decision trees "," k nearest neighbors "and" vector support machines "are high variance ML algorithms.

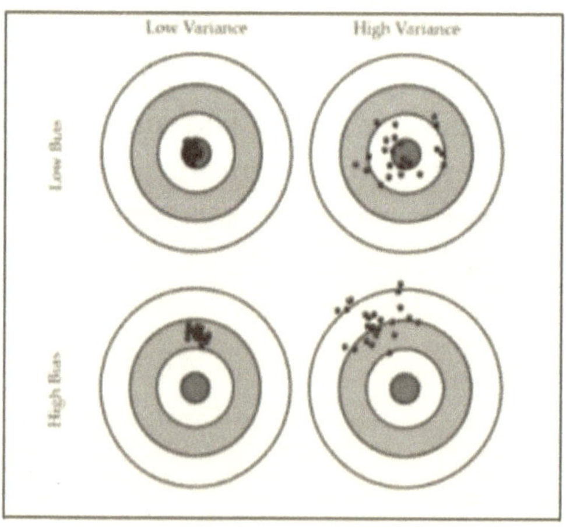

The interaction between bias and variance

In the context of statistical learning, 'bias' and 'variance' are inversely related. For a model with a high bias, the variance score is significantly reduced and vice versa. A compromise must be made between these two factors, driving the choice of model and its configuration to solve the intended problem by achieving a fine balance between the two. The right level of flexibility is critical to the efficiency and performance of any statistical learning technique in both the "regression" and "classification" environments. The interaction between "bias" and "variance" of the model and the subsequent "U-shape" in the test error is a major challenge.

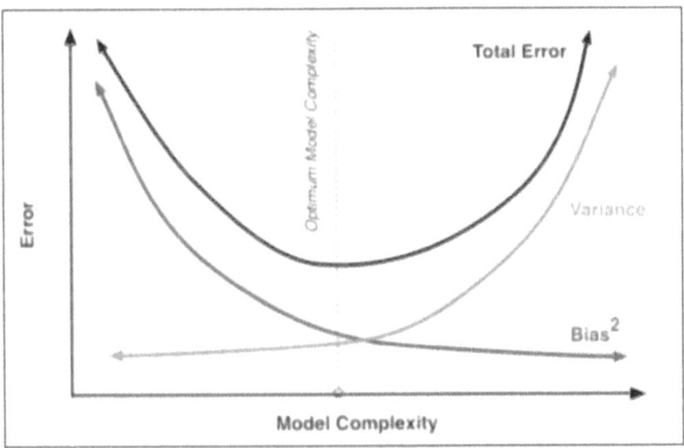

Chapter 3 : Machine learning algorithms

Machines can now learn and train on their own using previous calculations and underlying algorithms to produce high-quality, easily reproducible decisions and results. Machine learning has been around for a long time, but recent advances in machine learning algorithms have made it possible for machines to efficiently process and analyze large amounts of data. This is accomplished by using high speed and frequency automation to apply advanced and complex mathematical calculations to the machines. Today's sophisticated computer machines can quickly evaluate the massive amounts of data and deliver faster and more accurate results. Companies using machine learning algorithms have improved flexibility to tailor the training dataset to their business requirements and train the machines accordingly. With these custom machine learning algorithms, companies can identify potential hazards and growth opportunities. Working with artificial intelligence technology and cognitive technologies, machine learning algorithms are used to produce computers that are highly effective and highly efficient at handling large amounts of information or big data and produce highly accurate results.

Hundreds and thousands of machine learning algorithms have already been generated as this research field continues to expand. Here are some of the most commonly used algorithms, categorized by machine learning type:

To refresh your memory, guided learning is driven by the data scientists who provide guidance to teach the algorithm which conclusions to draw, using predefined training dataset. Guided learning requires information about all possible outputs from the algorithm and training data set that are already labeled with expected or correct results.
Let's take a look at the two most famous guided learning algorithms used to develop machine learning models, in detail!

Regression

The regression techniques fall under the supervised machine learning category. They help predict or describe a given numerical value based on the set of previous information, such as anticipating the cost of a property based on previous cost information for similar characteristics. Regression techniques range from simple (such as "linear regression") to complex (such as "regular linear regression", "polynomial regression", "decision trees", "random forest regression" and "neural networks", among others).

The simplest method is 'linear regression', using the 'mathematical equation (y = m * x + b) of the line to model the data set'. Multiple "data pairs (x, y)" can train a "linear" regression "model by calculating the position and slope of a line that can reduce the total distance between the data points and the line. In other words, calculating the" slope (m) "and" y-intercept (b) "has been used for a line that provides the highest approximation for data observations. The data relationships can be modeled using" linear predictive functions ", estimating unidentified model variables at based on the data These systems are called "linear models." Traditionally, if values of the "explanatory variables" or "predictors" are known, the conditional mean of the response would be used as the "affinity function" of those values. use of "conditional media" and other measures in linear models is very rare. Similar to any other form of "regression analysis sis" the "linear regression" works o ok on the "conditional probability distribution" of the responses instead of the joint probability distribution of the variables obtained with the multivariate analysis.

The most thoroughly researched form of regression analysis with wide applicability is "linear regression". This stems from the fact that models that rely linearly on their unidentified parameters are easy to work with compared to the models that are non-linearly related to their parameters. Because the statistical characteristics of the resulting predictors can be easily determined with a linear distribution. There are many useful applications of "linear regression" that can be divided into one of the following:

• If the goal is to generate forecasts and predictions or to reduce errors, the predictive model can be linked to an identified dataset and explanatory variables using a linear regression algorithm. Once the model is developed, new unresponsive input data can be easily predicted by the appropriate model.

• If the aim is to understand variations in the response variables that can be attributed to variations in the explanatory variables, "linear regression analysis" could be used to specifically quantify the relationship between the predictors and the response, to assess whether certain explanatory variables lack any linear relationship to the response. It can also be used to identify predictor subsets that contain data redundancy across response values.

The adaptation of most "linear regression models" is accomplished using the "least squares" approach. However, this model can also be fitted by significantly reducing the "lack of fit" in another standard (like the "least absolute deviation regression"), or by using a "punished version of the smallest square as done in the ridge regression. minimize (L2 standard penalty) and lasso regression (L1 standard penalty) ". In contrast, it is possible to use the "least squares" approach to fit machine learning models that are not linear. Therefore, although the terms "least squares" and "linear model" are closely related, they are not the same.

Multiple Linear Regression is generally the most common type of regression technique used in data science and most statistical tasks. As with the "linear regression" technique, there will be an output variable "Y" in "multiple linear regression". However, the difference now is that we will have numerous "X" or independent variables that generate predictions for "Y".

For example, a model developed to predict housing costs in Washington DC will be driven by the multiple linear regression technique. The cost of housing in Washington DC is the "Y" or dependent variable for the model. "X" or the independent variables for this model include data points such as proximity to public transport, training district, square meters and single rooms, which will ultimately determine the market price of the homes.

The mathematical equation for this model can be written as follows:

"Housing_price = β0 + β1 sq_foot + β2 dist_transport + β3 num_rooms"

Polynomial regression - Our models developed a straight line in the last two types of regression techniques. This straight line is the result of the connection between "X" and "Y" which is "linear" and the influence "X" has on "Y" does not change as the changing values of "X". Our model will lead in a row with a curve in "polynomial regression".

If we tried to fit a graph with nonlinear features using "linear regression", it would not yield the best fit for the nonlinear features. For example, the graph on the left is shown in the image below with the scatter plot showing an upward trend, but with a curve. A straight line does not work in this situation. Instead, we generate a line with a curve corresponding to the curve in our data with a polynomial regression, like the graph on the right in the figure below. The equation of a polynomial will appear as the linear equation, except that one or more of the "X" variables will be associated with a polynomial expression. For example,

'Y = mX2 + b'

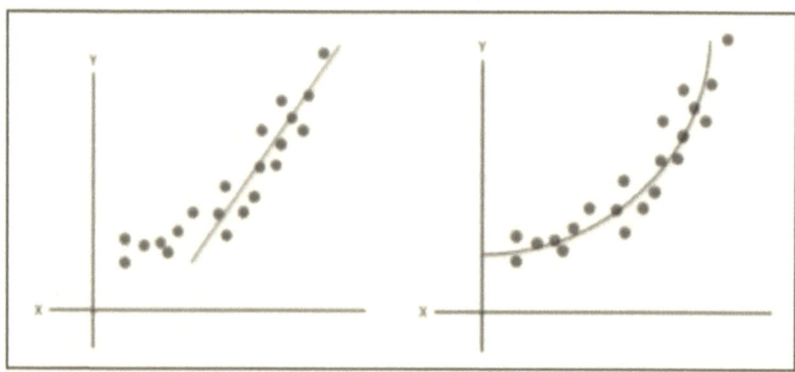

Another important "regression" technique for data researchers is "Support Vector Regression", which is most commonly used in "case classification". The concept here is to discover a line in space that divides data points into different categories. It is also used for regression. analysis It is a form of "binary classification" technique that is not associated with probability.

Ridge Regression is a widely used method for analyzing multi-collinear dataset. Depending on the characteristics of the data set, correct use of cam regression can reduce standard errors and significantly improve model accuracy.

Ridge regression can be useful if your data contains highly correlated independent variables. If you can predict an independent variable using another independent variable, your model will have a high risk of "multi-collinearity". For example, if you use variables that measure a person's height and weight; these variables in the model probably create "multi-collinearity".

Multicollinearity can potentially affect the accuracy of the predictions and predictions generated by the model. Consider the type of "predictive variables" used in the model to avoid multicollinearity, which can be caused by the type of data you are using, as well as the data collection method. Another reason could be the selection of a small variety of independent variables or the selection of independent variables was very limited, resulting in very similar data points.

Multicollinearity can also be caused by generating a very specific model. Note that there are more variables than data points in the model. If you have chosen to use a "linear" model "which worsened the multicollinearity of the model, you can try to implement a method of" cam regression ".

Ridge regression works to make the predictions more accurate by allowing a touch of bias in the model. This technique is also known as "regularization".

Another technique to improve the accuracy of the model is to "standardize" the independent variables. The simplest way is to reduce complexity by changing the values of certain independent variables to null. The approach is not just to change these independent variables to zero, but to implement a structure that rewards values closer to zero. This will decrease the coefficients, which will also decrease the complexity of the model, but the model will retain all its independent variables. This will give the model more bias, which is a tradeoff for greater accuracy of predictions. Another reduction technique is called "LASSO regression". A highly complementary "cam regression", "lasso regression" technique promotes the use of simpler and leaner models to generate predictions. In lasso regression, the model lowers the value of coefficients relatively stiffer. LASSO stands for the "least absolute crimp and selection operator". Data on our scatter plot, such as the average or median values of the data, is reduced to a more compact level. We use this when the model experiences a high multicollinearity, comparable to the "ridge regression" model.

A hybrid of "LASSO" and "cam regression" methods is known as "ElasticNet Regression". The main aim is to further improve the accuracy of the predictions generated by the "LASSO regression technique". "ElasticNet Regression" is a confluence of both "LASSO" and "ridge regression" techniques to reward smaller coefficient values. All three of these designs are available in the R and Python "Glmnet suite".

Bayesian regression models are useful if there is insufficient data or if the available data is poorly distributed. These regression models are developed from probability distributions rather than data points, which means that the resulting graph will appear as a bubble curve representing the variance with the most common values in the center of the curve. The dependent variable "Y" in "Bayesian regression" is not a valuation but a probability. Instead of predicting a value, we try to estimate the probability of an event. This is considered "frequentistic statistics" and this kind of statistics is based on the "Bayes theorem". Frequent statistics assume whether an event will occur and the likelihood that it will recur in the future.

"Conditional opportunity" is an integral part of the concept of "frequentist statistics". Conditional probability refers to the events on which the results are interdependent. Events can also be conditional, meaning the previous event can change the probability of the next event. Let's say you have a box of M & Ms and you want to understand the likelihood of getting different colors of the M & Ms out of the bag. If you have a set of 3 yellow M & M's and 3 blue M & M's, and you get a blue M & M on your first draw, chances are you will get a blue M & M on your next draw out of the box lower than the first draw. This is a classic example of "conditional opportunity". On the other hand, an independent event is the flip of a coin, meaning that the preceding coin cover does not change the probability of the next coin cover. Therefore, a coin flip is not an example of "conditional probability".

Classification

The "classification algorithm" in machine learning and statistics can be defined as the algorithm used to define the set of categories (subpopulations) under which the new input data can be grouped, based on the training data set composed of related data whose category is already identified. For example, all incoming emails can be grouped into the "spam" or "non-spam" category based on predefined rules. Likewise, a patient diagnosis can be categorized based on perceived characteristics of the patient, such as gender, blood type, prominent symptoms, family history for genetic diseases. Classification "can be considered as a type of pattern recognition technology. These individual hypotheses can be analyzed in a range of properties that can be easily quantified, also known as" explanatory variables or characteristics ". These can be classified as" categorical ", for example for different types of blood types. such as 'A +', 'O-' or 'ordinal' for example different types of measures such as large, small or 'whole values', for example the number of times a specific word is repeated in a text or "real values", for example length- and weight measurement Certain classifications work by comparing its previous observations using a "match or distance function".

Any machine learning algorithm that can implement classification, especially in the context of model implementation, is called "classifier". Very often the term "classifier" is used in the context of the math function, which is implemented by a "classification algorithm" and can assign new input to the correct category. In the field of statistics, the classification of data is often performed with "logistic regression", with the characteristics of the observations referred to as "explanatory variables" or "independent variables" or "regressors" and the categories used to generate predictions are known as "outcomes". These "outcomes" are considered the likely values of the dependent variable. In machine learning, "observations are often referred to as instances, the explanatory variables are referenced to similar characteristics (grouped in a characteristic vector), and the possible predictable categories are called classes".

The "Logistic regression" technique is "borrowed" by ML technology from the world of statistical analysis. "Logistic regression" is considered the simplest classification algorithm, although the term sounds like a technique of "regression", but it is not. "Logistic regression" produces estimates based on single or multiple input values for the probability of an event occurring. For example, a "logistic regression" will use a patient's symptoms, blood glucose, and family history as inputs to increase the likelihood of the patient developing diabetes. The model generates a prediction in the form of a probability from '1' to '10' where '10' means complete certainty. For the patient, if the expected chance is greater than 5, the prediction would be that they will have diabetes. If the predicted probability is less than 5, it is predicted that the patient will not develop diabetes. With logistic regression, a line graph can be created that can represent the "decision boundary".

It is widely used for binary classification tasks involving two different class values. Logistic regression is so called because of the fundamental statistical function underlying this technique called the "logistic function". Statisticians created the "logistics function", also known as the "sigmoid function", to define the characteristics of population growth in ecosystems, which continue to grow rapidly and approach the maximum carrying capacity of the environment. The logistic function is "an S-shaped curve that is able to take a real valued integer and map it to a value between '0' and '1', but never exactly at those limits, where 'e' is the basis of the natural log (Euler's number or the EXP) "and the numerical value you are actually going to transform is called the 'value'. '1 / (1 + e ^ value)'

Here is a chart with numbers from "-5 to 5" which has been converted by the logistics function to a range between 0 and 1.

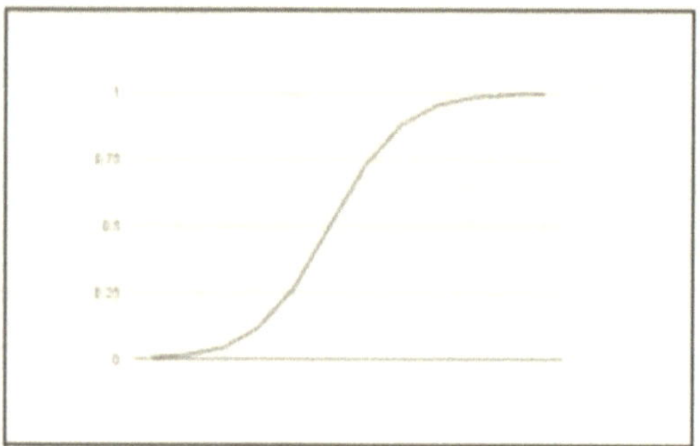

As with the "linear regression" technique, "logistic regression" uses an equation for data representation.

Input values (X) are grouped linearly to predict an output value (Y), using weights or coefficient values (represented as the symbol "Beta"). It differs mainly from the "linear regression" in that the modeled output value is usually binary (0 or 1) rather than a range of values.

Below is an example of the equation "logistic regression", where "the single input value coefficient (X) is represented by 'b1', the 'interception or distortion term' is the 'bo', and the 'expected result' is 'Y' Each column in the input data set has a related coefficient "b", which should be understood by learning the training data set. The actual model representation, which is stored in a file or in system memory, is "the coefficients in the equation (the beta values) ".

'y = e ^ (b0 + b1 * x) / (1 + e ^ (b0 + b1 * x))'

The coefficients of the "logistic regression" algorithm (the beta values) should be estimated from the training data. This can be accomplished using another statistical technique called "maximum probability estimation", a popular ML algorithm used using many other ML algorithms. "Maximum probability estimate" works by making certain assumptions about the distribution of the input data set.

An ML model that can predict a value closer to "0" for the "other class" and a value closer to "1" for the "standard class" can be obtained by using the best coefficients of the model. The underlying assumption for the most probable probability of the "logistic regression" technique is that "a search is attempting to find values for the coefficients that reduce the error in the probabilies estimated by the model with respect to the input data set (eg Probability of '0' if the input data is not the standard class) ".

Without going into mathematical details, suffice it to say that you will "use a minimization algorithm to optimize the values of the best coefficients from your training data set". In practice, this can be achieved using an effective "numerical optimization algorithm" (for example, the "Quasi-Newton" technique).

Generate predictions using logistic regression

Here you can easily plug the measurements into the "logistic regression" equation and calculate the result to generate predictions with the "logistic regression" model. Let's look at an example to reinforce this concept. Let's assume there is a model that can generate predictions if an individual is male or female depending on fictional values of their height. If the height value for a person is set to 150 cm, is the person predicted to be a man or a woman? Assuming we have already discovered the values of the coefficients "b0 = -100" and "b1 = 0.6". Using the equation above, the probability of a man having a height of 150 cm or "P (male | height = 150)" can be easily calculated. The EXP () function is used for "e" because if you log this instance into your spreadsheet, you can use this:

"Y = e ^ (b0 + b1 * X) / (1 + e ^ (b0 + b1 * X))"
"Y = exp (-100 + 0.6 * 150) / (1 + EXP (-100 + 0.6 * X))"
'Y = 0.0000453978687'

Or an almost "0" chance is the gender of that specific person. In theory, the opportunity can be easily used. But since this is a "classification" algorithm and we want a sharp result, the probabilities can be tagged on a binary class value. In front of For example, the model can predict "0" if "p (male) <0.51" and predict "1" if "p (male)> = 0.5". Now that you know how to generate predictions using "logistic regression", you can easily pre-process the training data set to get the most out of this technique. The assumptions made about the distribution and relationships within the dataset with the "logistic regression" technique are almost identical to the assumptions made in the "linear regression" technique.

Much research has been done to define these hypotheses and to use accurate probabilistic and statistical language. It is recommended to use these as thumb rules or guidelines and try different data preparation processes.

The ultimate goal of machine learning "predictive modeling" initiatives is to generate highly accurate predictions rather than analysis of results. All things considered, some assumptions could be broken if the designed model is stable and delivers high performance.

• "Binary output variable": this may be obvious as we have discussed it before, but "logistic regression" is specially designed for "binary (two class) classification" issues. This will generate predictions for the probability of a standard class instance that can be tagged in a rating of "0" or "1".

• "Remove Noise": Logistic regression does not assume errors in the "output variable (" y ")", therefore the cases of "outliers and possibly mis-classified" should be removed from the training data set.

• "Gaussian distribution": Logistic regression can be considered as a kind of "linear algorithm but with a non-linear transformation on the output". A line connection between the output and input variables is also assumed. Data transformations of the input variables can lead to a more accurate model with a higher ability to reveal the linear relationships of the data set. For example, to better reveal these relationships, we could use "log", "root", "Box-Cox" and other single-variable transforms.

• "Remove correlated inputs": if you have several highly correlated inputs, the model may be "over-fit", similar to the "linear regression" technique.
To address this problem, you can "calculate the pairwise correlations between all input data points and remove the highly correlated input".

• "Do not converge": it is likely that the "expected probability estimate" method trained on the coefficients will not converge. It can happen if the dataset contains multiple strongly correlated inputs or if there is very limited data (eg loads of "0" in the input data).

"Naïve Bayes classification algorithm" is another "classification" learning algorithm with a wide variety of applications. It is a classification method derived from the Bayes' theorem, which assumes that predictors are independent of each other. Simply put, a 'Naïve Bayes classifier' assumes that 'all functions in a class have nothing to do with the existence of any other function in that class'. For example, if input data has an image of a fruit that is green, round, and about 10 inches in diameter, the model may consider the input to be a watermelon. Although these characteristics are based on each other or on the presence of a specific characteristic, all characteristics independently contribute to the likelihood that the image of the fruit is that of a watermelon, therefore it is called "naive". "Naive Bayes model" for large amounts of data sets is relatively easy to construct and extremely effective.

"Naïve Bayes" is said to have surpassed even the most advanced classification techniques, along with the simplicity of development. "Bayes' theorem" may also provide the means to calculate the posterior probability "P (c | x)" using "P (c), P (x) and P (x)". Based on the comparison in the image below, where the probability of "c" can be calculated if "x" has already occurred.

"P (c | x)" is the rear probability of "class (c, target)" provided by the "predictor (x, attributes)". "P (c)" is the earlier probability of the class. "P (x | c)" is the probability of the class given by the predictor. "P (x)" is the predictor's previous probability.

$$P(c \mid x) = \frac{P(x \mid c)\,P(c)}{P(x)}$$

where $P(c \mid x)$ is the Posterior Probability, $P(x \mid c)$ is the Likelihood, $P(c)$ is the Class Prior Probability, and $P(x)$ is the Predictor Prior Probability.

$$P(c \mid X) = P(x_1 \mid c) \times P(x_2 \mid c) \times \cdots \times P(x_n \mid c) \times P(c)$$

Here is an example to better explain the application of the "Bayes theorem". The image below presents the data on the problem of identifying suitable weather days to play golf. The columns show the weather characteristics of the day and the rows contain individual entries. Considering the first row of the dataset, it can be concluded that the weather will be too hot and humid with rain, so the day is not suitable for golfing. Now the primary assumption is that all of these characteristics or predictors are independent of each other. The other assumption made here is that all predictors potentially have the same effect on the result. This means that if the day were windy, it would be relevant to the decision to play golf like the rain. In this example, the variable (c) is the class (playing golf) representing the decision whether it is suitable for golf again and variable (x) represents the characteristics or predictors.

	OUTLOOK	TEMPERATURE	HUMIDITY	WINDY	PLAY GOLF
0	Rainy	Hot	High	False	No
1	Rainy	Hot	High	True	No
2	Overcast	Hot	High	False	Yes
3	Sunny	Mild	High	False	Yes
4	Sunny	Cool	Normal	False	Yes
5	Sunny	Cool	Normal	True	No
6	Overcast	Cool	Normal	True	Yes
7	Rainy	Mild	High	False	No
8	Rainy	Cool	Normal	False	Yes
9	Sunny	Mild	Normal	False	Yes
10	Rainy	Mild	Normal	True	Yes
11	Overcast	Mild	High	True	Yes
12	Overcast	Hot	Normal	False	Yes
13	Sunny	Mild	High	True	No

Types of "Naive Bayes classification"

• "Multinomial Naive Bayes" - This is widely used to classify documents, for example, which category a document belongs to: beauty, technology, politics, etc. The frequency of the sentences in the document is considered to be the characteristics or predictors of the classifier.
• "Bernoulli Naive Bayes" - This is almost identical to the "Multinomial Naive Bayes", but the predictors used here are the "Boolean variables". For example, depending on whether or not a selective phrase appears in the text, the parameters used to predict the class variable can be a yes or no value.
• "Gaussian Naive Bayes" - When the predictors do not differ and have very similar or continuous values, it can be assumed that these values are obtained from a Gaussian distribution.
Applications of "Naïve Bayes"
• "Real-Time Prediction": Naive Bayes learns super fast from the input data and can be seamlessly used to generate real-time predictions.

• "Multi-class prediction": This algorithm is also widely used to generate predictions for multiple classes at once. It allows the prediction of the probability of different classes of the target variable.

• "Text Classification / Spam Filtering / Sentiment Analysis": The "Naive Bayes Classifications" are widely used in text classification models because of the ability to address issues with multiple classes of the target variable and the rule of autonomy. This algorithm has reported higher success rates than any other algorithm. As a result, it is often used to identify spam emails and sentiment analysis by identifying favorable and negative consumer sentiments on the social media platforms.

• "Recommendation System": "Naive Bayes Classifier" and "Collaborative Filtering" can be combined to generate a "Recommendation System" that uses ML and data mining methods to filter hidden data and generate insight as to whether the customer has a particular item would prefer or product.

Chapter 4 : Neural network learning models

Artificial Neural Networks or (ANN) have been developed and designed to mimic the path of communication in the human brain. In the human body, billions of neurons are all linked together and travel up through the spine and into the brain. They are attached to each other by root-like nodes that send messages one by one through the neurons throughout the chain until they reach the brain. These systems "learn" to perform tasks by looking at examples, usually without any of the task-specific rules configured. For example, they can learn to distinguish images containing dogs using the image recognition technology by evaluating sample photos manually marked as "dog" or "no dog" and using the results to locate dogs in other images. These systems can
achieve this even without previous knowledge of dogs such as fur, tails and dog-like faces. Rather, they are capable of automatically producing identification functions based on the samples they have been trained on.

An ANN functions as a collection of linked units or nodes called "artificial neurons" that resemble the biological neurons of the human brain. Each link can transmit a signal to connected neurons, similar to the synapses in the human brain. An "artificial neuron" that receives a signal can then process it and then transfer it to the connected neurons. When implementing the ANN, the "signal" at a junction will be a real number and the outcome of each neuron will be calculated using a certain "non-linear function" of the sum of the inputs. The connections are known as "edges". Generally, the neurons and "edges" are marked with a value or weight that will be optimized with learning. The weight increases or decreases the strength of the signal received by the connected neuron. Concepts are formed and distributed through the subnetwork of shared neurons. Neurons can be set with threshold limits, so that a signal is only sent when the accumulated signal exceeds the set threshold. Neurons are usually composed of several layers, which are able to uniquely transform their input. Signals are passed from the first layer called "input layer" to the last layer called "output layer", sometimes after the layers have been crossed several times.

The ANN model's original goal was to solve problems reached by a human brain. However, over time, the focus is on performing selected tasks, resulting in a shift from the original goal. ANNs can be used for a variety of tasks such as "computer vision, speech recognition, machine translation, social media filtering, game boards and video games, medical diagnostics and even painting".

The most common ANN works on a unidirectional flow of information and is called "Feedforward ANN". However, ANN is also capable of bidirectional and cyclical information flows to achieve the state balance. ANNs learn from previous cases by adjusting the connected weights and rely on fewer previous assumptions. This learning can be supervised or unsupervised. With guided learning, each input pattern will result in the correct ANN output. To reduce the error between the given output and the output generated by ANN, the weights can be varied. For example, enhanced learning, a form of "guided learning", informs the ANN if the generated output is correct instead of directly delivering the correct output. On the other hand, unsupervised learning provides multiple input patterns for the ANN, and then the ANN itself explores the relationship between these patterns and learns to categorize them accordingly. ANNs with a combination of guided and unaccompanied learning are also available.

To solve data-heavy problems where the algorithm or rules are unknown or difficult to understand, ANNs are very useful due to their data structure and non-linear calculations. ANNs are robust against multi-variable errors and can easily process complex information in parallel. ANN's black box model is a major drawback, however, making them unsuitable for issues that require a deep understanding and understanding of the actual process.

Components of ANNs

• Neurons - ANNs retained the biological idea of artificial neurons receiving input, combined with their internal state and threshold value if available, using an "activation function" and generating output using an "output function". Any kind of data, including images and files, can be used as the first input. The final results obtained may be the recognition of an object in a photo. The important feature of the "enable function" is that as the input values continue to change, this ensures a seamless transition, meaning that a small change in the input will result in a small change in the output.
• Connections and Weights - The ANN consists of connections that use the output of one neuron as input for an associated neuron. Each connection is assigned a "weight" that represents the relative meaning of the signal. There can be numerous input and output connections for a specific neuron.
• Propagation function - The "propagation function" can calculate the input to a neuron from the output of its predecessors and their connections, in the form of a "weighted sum". A "bias term" can be applied to the "propagation result". Backpropagation can be defined as a method of adjusting the connection weights to adjust for each error that occurs during the learning process. The amount of errors is easily distributed among the connections. Theoretically, "backprop" calculates the gradient of the "cost function" associated with the weight of the given state. The weight can be updated via the "stochastic gradient descent" or other techniques, including "Extreme Learning Machines", "No-prop" network, "weightless" network and "non-connective" neural network.

Hyperparameter of ANN

A "hyperparameter" can be defined as a parameter that is set before the actual start of the learning process. The parameter values are obtained by the learning process. For example, learning speed, batch size and number of hidden layers. Some "hyper parameter values" may depend on other "hyper parameter values". For example, the size of certain layers may depend on the total number of layers. The "learning rate" for each observation indicates the magnitude of the corrective actions the model needs to compensate for any errors. A higher learning rate reduces the time it takes to train the model, but results in reduced accuracy. On the other hand, a slower pace of learning increases the time it takes to train the model, but may result in higher accuracy. Optimizations "such as" Quickprop "are mainly aimed at accelerating the minimization of errors, while other improvements are primarily aimed at increasing the reliability of the output. Refinements" use an "adaptive learning speed" that can be increased or decreased, if applicable, to avoid oscillation within the network, including the alternation of connection weights, and to help increase the convergence speed. The principle of momentum allows the balance between the gradient and the previous change to be weighted, so that the weight adjustment depends to some extent on the previous change. The gradient is emphasized by the momentum close to "0", while the last change is emphasized by a value close to "1".

Neural network training with data pipeline

A neural network can be defined as "a function that learns the expected output for a given input from training data sets". Unlike the "artificial neural network", the "neural network" contains only one neuron, also called "perceptron". It is a simple and fundamental mechanism that can be implemented with basic math. The main distinction between traditional programming and a neural network is that computers running on a neural network learn from the provided training data set to determine the parameters (weights and biases) themselves, without needing any human assistance. Algorithms such as "backpropagation" and "gradient descent" can be used to determine the

parameters. It can be argued that the computer tries to increase or decrease each parameter a little, hoping to find the optimal combination of parameters, to minimize the error compared to the training data set.

Computer programmers will typically "define a pipeline for data to flow through their machine learning model." Each phase of the pipeline uses the data generated from the previous phase after processing the data as needed. The word "pipeline" can be a bit misleading because it indicates a one-way flow of data when in reality the machine learning pipelines are "cyclic and iterative" as each phase would be repeated to eventually produce an effective algorithm.

While programmers want to develop a machine learning model, they work in selected development environments that are tailored to include "Statistics" and "Machine Learning" such as Python and R. These environments allow training and testing of the models using a single "sandboxed" environment while relatively fewer lines of code are written. This is great for developing interactive prototypes that can be brought to market quickly, rather than developing low-latency production systems.

The primary goal of developing a machine learning pipeline is to build a model with the following functions:

• Must allow a reduction in system latency.

• Integration but loose link with other components of the model, such as data storage systems, reporting functionalities and "Graphical User Interface (GUI)".

• Must allow both horizontal and vertical scalability.

• Must be message driven, which means that the model must be able to communicate by transferring "asynchronous, non-blocking messages".

• Ability to generate effective calculations for data set management.

• Must be able to withstand system errors and be able to recover with minimal to no supervision, also known as failure management.

• Must be able to support "batch" and "real-time" processing of the input data.

Conventionally, data pipelines require "one night batch processing," which means that the data must be collected, sent with an "enterprise message bus", and then processed to generate pre-calculated results and guidelines for future transactions. While this model has proven to work in certain industrial sectors, in others, and especially when it comes to machine learning models, batch processing is not a challenge. The image below shows a machine learning data pipeline as applied to a real-time business problem where attributes and projections depend on the time it takes to generate the results. For example, product recommendation systems used by Amazon, an arrival time estimation system used by Lyft, a system to recommend potential new links used by LinkedIn, search engines used by Airbnb, among others.

The swimlane diagram above consists of two explicitly specified components:
1. "Online Model Analytics": The top swimlane of the image shows the elements of the application required for operation. It shows where the model is used to make real-time decisions.
2. "Offline Data Discovery": The lower swim lane shows the learning element of the model, which is used to analyze historical data and generate the machine learning model using the "batch processing" method.
There are 8 fundamental stages in creating a data pipeline, which are shown in the image below and explained in detail here:

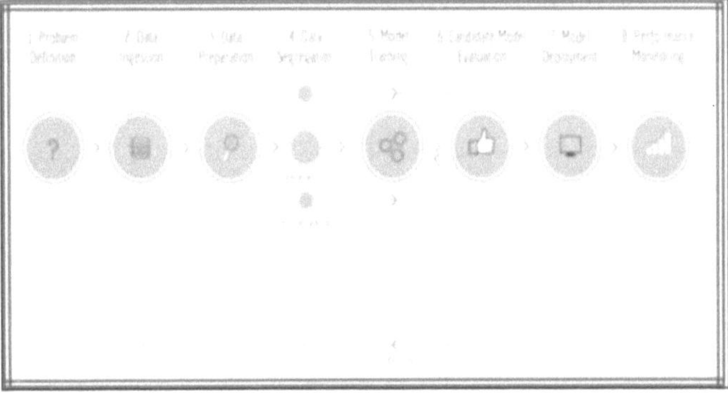

1. Problem definition

At this stage, the business problem to be solved using a machine learning model is identified and documented with all relevant details.

2. Data recording

The first stage of any machine learning workflow is entering input data to a database server. The important thing to remember is that the data is recorded unedited and not modified so that we can have an unchanging record of the original data set. Data can be provided from various sources that can be obtained on request or sent from other systems. "NoSQL document databases" are best suited to store huge amounts of defined and tagged and disorganized raw data, which evolve quickly because they don't have to stick to a predefined schedule. It even provides "distributed", scalable and replicated data "storage".
Offline
Data will flow in the "offline" layer to the raw data store via an "Ingestion Service", which is a "composite orchestration service capable of encapsulating data collection and persistence". A repository model is used internally to communicate with a data service that interacts with the data store in exchange. When you store the data in the database, a unique batch ID is given to the data set, enabling the data to be retrieved effectively and the data to be tracked and monitored end-to-end.

To be computationally efficient, the recording of the data is divided into two folds.

• The first is a specific pipeline for each data set, so that each of the data sets can be processed separately and simultaneously.

• The second aspect is that data can be broken down within each pipeline to make the most of a variety of server cores, processors, and perhaps even the entire server.

Dividing the preparation of data across different vertical and horizontal pipelines will reduce the total time required to complete the tasks.

The Intake Service would operate at regular intervals based on a pre-determined schedule (one or more times a day) or upon encountering a trigger. A topic will disconnect producers (data source) from processors, which would be the data pipeline for this example, so when the source data is collected, the "producer system" sends a notification to the "broker" and then the "embedded notification" service will respond by generating the recording of the data The "Notification Service" would also inform the "broker" that the processing of the original dataset has been successfully completed and now the dataset is stored in the database.

"Online"

The "Online Ingestion Service" provides access to the "streaming architecture" of the online layer as it would decouple and manage the data flow from the source to the processing and storage components by providing consistent, high-quality, low-latency functionalities. It also works as a "data bus" at the company level. Data would be stored on a long-term "Raw Data Storage", which also serves as an intermediary layer for the subsequent online streaming service for further processing in real time. Such techniques used in this case can be, for example, "Apache Kafka (pub / sub message system)" and "Apache Flume (data set to the long-term database)". A variety of other similar techniques are available and can be selectively applied based on the company's technology stack.

3. Data preparation

Once the information is included, a centralized pipeline would be produced that can evaluate the state of the data, meaning it would look for format variations, outliers, patterns, inaccurate, incomplete or distorted information and correct any anomalies in the process. The feature engineering process is also included in this phase. The 3 main characters of a feature pipeline as shown in the image below are: "extraction, transformation and selection".

Phase	Input	Output
Extract	Raw data	Feature
Transform	Feature	Feature
Select	List<Feature>	List<Feature>

Since this is often the most complicated part of any machine learning project, it is essential to introduce suitable design patterns. In the context of coding, this implies using a factory technique to produce features based on certain shared abstract function behaviors, and a strategy pattern for selecting the right features at the time of execution can be considered a logical approach. It is important to take into account the composition and reusability of the pipeline when structuring the feature extractors and transformers.

The selection of functionalities can be attributed to the caller or can be automated. For example, a "chi-square statistical test" can be applied to classify the impact of each function on the concept label, while the low impact functions are discarded before the model is trained. To achieve this, some "selector APIs" can be identified. In any case, each function set must be assigned a unique ID to ensure that the functions used as model input and for impact scoring are consistent. In general, it is necessary to merge a data preparation pipeline into a series of immutable transformations, which can be easily combined. Now the importance of "testing and high code coverage" becomes a critical factor in the success of the model.

4. Separation of data

The primary goal of the machine learning model is to develop a high-accuracy model based on the quality of the forecasts and predictions for information derived from the new input data, which was not part of the training data set. Therefore, the available labeled data set will be used as a "proxy" for future unknown input data by splitting the data into training and test data sets. Many approaches are available to split the dataset and some of the most commonly used techniques are:

• Use the standard or custom ratio to divide the dataset into two subsets sequentially to ensure that there is no overlap in the order in which the data appears from the source. For example, you can select the first 75% of the data to train the model and the resulting 25% of the data to test the accuracy of the model.

• Splitting the dataset into training and testing a subset with a standard or adjusted ratio with any seed. For example, you can choose any 75% of the dataset to train the model and the remaining 25% of the random dataset to test the model.

• Use any of these techniques ("sequential vs. random") and then mix the data within each data subset.

• Use a custom injected approach to splitting the data when comprehensive control of data separation is required. Technically, the data segregation phase is not considered an independent machine learning pipeline, but an "API" or tool must be provided to support this phase. In order to return the required datasets, the following 2 phases ("model training" and "model assessment") must be able to call this "API". Regarding the organization of the code, a "strategy pattern" is required so that the "caller service" can select the appropriate algorithm at runtime and the ability to inject percentage or random seed is required. The "API" must also be prepared to return the information with or without labels, to train and test the model, respectively. A warning can be created and passed along with the dataset to protect the "caller service" from defining parameters that can cause uneven data distribution.

5. Model training

The model pipelines are always "offline" and the schedule ranges from a few hours to just one run per day, based entirely on the complexity of the application. Training can also be started on time and event, and not just by the system planners.

It contains many libraries of machine learning algorithms, such as 'linear regression, ARIMA, k-means, decision trees' and many more, which are designed to provide facilities for rapid production of new model types and to make the models interchangeable. Embedding is also important for the integration of "third party APIs" using the "facade pattern" (at this stage it may also be called the "Python Jupyter notebook"). You have several choices for "parallelization":

• A specialized pipeline for individual models is usually the simplest method, meaning that all models can be used at the same time.

• Another approach would be to duplicate the training data set, ie the data set can be divided and each data set will contain a replica of the model. This approach is preferred for the models that need all fields of an instance to perform the calculations, for example "LDA", "MF".

• Another approach could be to parallelize the entire model, which means that the model can be separated and each partition can be responsible for preserving a fraction of the variables. This approach is best suited for linear machine learning models, such as "Linear Regression", "Support Vector Machine".

• Finally, a hybrid strategy can also be used using a combination of one or more of the above approaches.

It is important to train the model, taking into account fault tolerance. Data checkpoints and failures on training partitions should also be considered. For example, if each partition is not due to a temporary problem, such as a timeout, each partition can be retrained.

Neural network training approaches

As with most traditional machine learning models, Neural Networks can be trained using supervised and unaccompanied learning algorithms, as described below:

Guided training

Both inputs and outputs are provided to the machine as part of the guided training effort. The network then processes the inputs and compares the generated outputs with the expected outputs. Errors are then passed through the model, causing the model to adjust the weights that control the network. This cycle is repeated over and over and the weights are constantly changing. The data set that enables learning is called the "training set". The same data set is processed multiple times while the weights of a relationship are continuously improved by training a network.

Current enterprise network development packages provide means for monitoring the convergence of an artificial neural network at its capacity to predict the correct outcome. These resources allow the training routine to continue for days until the model reaches the required statistical level or accuracy. However, some networks cannot learn. This may be due to the lack of concrete information in the input data from which the expected output is obtained. Networks will also not converge if there is insufficient quantity and quality of data available to provide full learning. Sufficient volume of the dataset must be available to test part of the dataset. Most multi-node layered networks can remember and store large amounts of data. To monitor the network to determine if the system only stores training data in a meaningless way, supervised learning requires that a set of data be stored and used to evaluate the system once it has been trained.

To avoid insignificant memorization, the number of processing elements should be reduced. If a network cannot easily solve the problem, the developer must evaluate the input and output, the number of layers and its elements, the connections between these layers, the data transfer and training functionalities, and even the original input weights. These adaptations necessary to develop an effective network include the approach in which the "art" of neural networks takes place. Several algorithms are required to provide the iterative feedback needed for weight adjustments during exercise. The most common technique is "backward-error propagation", more often called "back-propagation". To ensure that the network is not "overtrained", supervised training should include an intuitive and informed analysis of the model. An artificial neural network is initially configured with current statistical data trends. It should then continue to learn other data aspects that could be incorrect from a general point of view. If the model is properly trained and no additional learning is required, the weights can be "frozen" if necessary. On some models, this completed network is converted to hardware to increase the processing speed of the model. Certain machines do not lock, but continue to learn through their use in the production environment.

Uncontrolled training

The network only comes with inputs and not with expected results, in "unattended or adaptive" training. The model must then determine the functionality for grouping the input data. This is often referred to as "self-organization or adaptation." Supervised learning is currently not well understood. This adaptation to the environment is the promise that allows robots to continuously learn independently when they encounter new circumstances and unique settings. The real world is full of situations where training data sets are not available to solve a problem. Some of these scenarios include military intervention, which may require new fighting techniques as well as weapons and ammunition. Because of this unexpected element of existence and the human desire to be equipped to handle any situation, the ongoing study and hope for this discipline continues. The vast majority of the neural network is currently performed in models with guided learning.
Teuvo Kohonen, an electrical engineer from Helsinki University of Technology, is one of the pioneering researchers in unsupervised training. He has built a self-organizing network, also known as an "auto-associator", that can learn without any knowledge of the expected outcome. It consists of a single layer with numerous connections in a network that looks unusual. For these connections, the weights must be initialized and the inputs must be normalized. The neurons are organized in a "way of winning everything". Kohonen is constantly researching networks designed differently from conventional feed forward and back propagation methods. Kohonen's research focuses on the organization of neurons in the network of the model.

Neurons within a domain are "topologically organized". Topology is defined as' a branch of mathematics that examines how it can map from one space to another without changing the geometrical configuration. An example of a topological organization are the three-dimensional groups that are common in the mammalian brain. Kohonen noted that the absence of topology in neural network design makes these artificial neural networks merely a simple abstraction of the true neural networks in the human brain. Advanced self-learning networks may become possible as this research progresses.

6. Candidate model evaluation

The model evaluation phase is always "offline". By comparing the predictions generated with the test data set with the actual data values using different performance indicators and measures, the "predictive performance" of a model can be measured. To generate a prediction of future input data, the "best" model from the test subset is preferred. An evaluator library consisting of several evaluators can be designed to generate accuracy statistics, such as "ROC curve" or "PR curve", which can also be stored in a data store against the model. Once again, the same techniques are applied to enable flexible combining and switching between assessors.

The "Model Evaluation Service" will request the test data set from the "Data Segregation API" to organize training and testing of the model. In addition, corresponding assessors will be requested for the model from the "Model Candidate repository". The test findings are sent back to and stored in the repository. To develop the final machine learning model, an incremental procedure, hyperparameter optimization and regularization methods would be used. The best model would be considered deployable in the production environment and eventually be brought to market. The implementation information is published by the "reporting service".

7. Model implementation

The highest performance machine learning model is flagged for implementation to generate "offline (asynchronous)" and "online (synchronous)" predictions. It is recommended to deploy multiple models at the same time to ensure that the transition from legacy to the current model is smooth, meaning that the services should continue to meet forecast requirements without expiration while the new model is being implemented.

Historically, the biggest implementation problem has been the coding language needed to operate the models, not the same as the coding language used to build them. It is difficult to operationalize a Python or R based model in production with languages such as "C ++, C # or Java". This also leads to a significant reduction in performance in terms of speed and accuracy of the deployed model. This issue can be addressed in a number of areas, as noted below:

6. Candidate model evaluation

The model evaluation phase is always "offline". By comparing the predictions generated with the test data set to the actual data values using different performance indicators and measurements, the "predictive performance" of a model can be measured. To generate a prediction of future input data, the "best" model from the test subset is preferred. An evaluator library consisting of multiple evaluators can be designed to generate accuracy statistics, such as "ROC curve" or "PR curve", which can also be stored in a data store against the model. Again, the same techniques are applied to enable flexible combining and switching between assessors.

The "Model Evaluation Service" will request the test dataset from the "Data Segregation API" to organize training and testing of the model. In addition, corresponding assessors for the model will be requested from the "Model Candidate repository". The test results are sent back to and stored in the repository. An incremental procedure, hyperparameter optimization and regularization methods would be used to develop the final machine learning model. The best model is considered to be usable in the production environment and eventually brought to the market. The implementation information is published by the "reporting service".

7. Model implementation

The highest performance machine learning model is flagged for implementation to generate 'offline (asynchronous)' and 'online (synchronous)' predictions. It is recommended to deploy multiple models at the same time to ensure a smooth transition from legacy to the current model, meaning that the services must continue to meet forecast requirements without expiring while the new model is deployed.

Historically, the biggest implementation problem was the coding language needed to operate the models, not the same as the coding language used to build them. It is difficult to operationalize a Python or R based model in production with languages such as "C ++, C # or Java". This also significantly reduces performance in terms of speed and accuracy of the deployed model. This issue can be addressed in a number of areas, as noted below:

After the models are deployed, they can be used to score based on the job data provided by the previous pipelines or provided directly by a "customer service". The models must generate predictions with the same accuracy and high performance, both online and offline.

Offline

The "scoring service" would be optimized in the offline layer for a large data volume to achieve high performance and generate "fire and forget" predictions. A model can send an "asynchronous request" to start scoring, but it must wait for the batch score process to complete and access the batch score results before starting the scoring. The "scoring service" prepares the data, produces the functions and retrieves additional functions from the "Feature Data Store". The results of the score are stored in the "Score Data Store" once the score is completed. The "broker" is informed of the completion of the score by receiving notification from the service. This event is detected by the model, which then continues to collect the score results.

"Online"

In "online" mode, a "customer" sends a request to the "Online Scoring Service". The customer may request to invoke a specific version of the model so that the "Model Router" can inspect the request and then transfer the request to the corresponding model. According to request and in the same way as the offline layer, the "customer service" will also prepare the data, produce the functions and, if necessary, retrieve additional functions from the "Feature Data Store". After scoring, the scores are stored in the "Score Data Store" and then sent back to "customer service" via the network. Entirely depending on the use case, results can be delivered asynchronously to the "customer", which means that the results scored are reported independently of the request using one of two methods below:

• Push: After the scores have been achieved, they are pushed to the "customer" in the form of a "report".

• Poll: After the scores are produced, they are stored in a "low-latency database" and the client will poll the database regularly to retrieve any existing predictions.

There are a number of techniques listed below that can be used to reduce the time it takes the system to deliver the scores once the request is received:
• The input functions can be stored in a "low-read latency in-memory data store".
• The predictions already calculated using an "offline batch scoring" task can be cached for easy access, as determined by the use case, since "offline predictions" may lose relevance.

9. Performance monitoring

A very well-defined "performance monitoring solution" is required for each machine learning model. For the "customer service model", some of the data points you may want to observe are:
• "Model identification"
• "Implementation date and time"
• The "number of times" the model has been operated.
• The "average, min and max" of time taken to operate the model.
• The "distribution of functions" used.
• The difference between the "predicted or expected results" and the "actual or observed results".
These metadata can be calculated throughout the model scoring process and then used to monitor model performance.

Another "offline pipeline" is the "Performance Monitoring Service", which is notified when a new forecast is made and then continues to evaluate performance while maintaining the score result and generating relevant notifications. The assessment will be performed by comparing the scoring results with the output created by the training set of the data pipeline. Several methods can be used to implement basic performance monitoring of the model. Some of the commonly used methods are "logging analytics" such as "Kibana", "Grafana" and "Splunk".

An underperforming model that is unable to generate predictions at high speed will activate the score results produced by the previous model to maintain the resilience of the machine learning solution. A strategy is applied to be incorrect rather than late, which means that if the model takes a longer period to calculate a given characteristic, it will be replaced by an earlier model instead of the block prediction. In addition, the scoring results will be linked to the actual results if they are accessible. This means that the precision of the model is continuously measured and at the same time any sign of deterioration of the execution speed can be corrected by returning to the previous model. To link the different versions, a "chain of responsibility pattern" could be used. Monitoring the performance of the models is an ongoing method, as a simple prediction change can lead to a model structure being reorganized. Remember, the benefits of machine learning models are determined by the ability to generate predictions and predictions with high accuracy and speed to contribute to the company's success.

Applications of neural network models

Image processing and character recognition: ANNs have an inherent ability to consume different inputs, which can be processed to derive both hidden and complex, nonlinear relationships, ANNs play an important role in image and character recognition. Character recognition such as handwriting adds various applicability in identifying fraudulent monetary transactions and even national security matters. Image recognition is a huge field with extensive applications ranging from facial recognition on the social media platforms such as "Instagram" and "Facebook", as well as in the medical sciences for cancer detection in patients to satellite imaging for environmental research and agricultural use. ANN developments have now laid the foundation for "deep neural networks" that serve as the basis for "deep learning" technology.
Forecasting: In day-to-day business decisions, for example sales forecasts, capital distribution between raw materials, capacity utilization), economic and monetary policy, finance and stock markets, forecasting is the instrument of choice across the industrial spectrum. For example, predicting stock prices is a complicated issue with many underlying variables that can remain hidden in the depth of big data or readily available. Traditional forecasting models often have several limitations to account for these complicated, nonlinear associations. Due to the ability to model and extract hidden features and interactions, the implementation of ANNs can properly provide a reliable solution to the problem.

ANNs are also free from any restrictions on input and residual distributions, unlike traditional prediction models. For example, continued progress in this area has resulted in recent advances in the predictive use of "LSTM" and "Recurrent Neural Networks" to generate projections from the model. For example, predict the weather; currency systems used by "Citibank London" are powered by neural networks.

Chapter 5 : Learning through uniform convergence

The most fundamental question of the theory of statistical learning is to characterize the learning ability of the model. In the case models driven by "supervised classification and regression techniques", it can be assumed that learnability equals the "uniform convergence" of empirical risk to population risk. This means that if a problem can be trained, it can only be learned by minimizing the empirical risk of the data. "Uniform convergence in probability", in the context of statistical asymptotic theory and probability theory, is a type of convergence in probability. It implies that within a given event family, the empirical frequencies of all events converge to their theoretical probabilities under certain circumstances. "Uniform convergence in probability" as part of statistical learning theory is widely applicable to machine learning. Uniform convergence is defined as "a mode of convergence of characteristics stronger than point-wise convergence, in the mathematical analysis area".

In 1995 Vapnik published the "General Setting of Learning", which deals with the topic of statistical learnability. The general learning environment deals with learning difficulties. Conventionally, a learning problem can be defined using a 'hypothesis class' H', an instance series' Z '(with a sigma algebra) and an objective function (eg Loss or cost)' ie 'f: $H \times Z \rightarrow R$ " . This theory can be used "to minimize a population risk functionally over some hypothesis class H, where the distribution D of Z is unknown, based on sample z1, ..., zm drawn from D".

"$F(h) = E_{Z \sim D}[f(h; Z)]$"

This general setting includes "supervised classification and regression" techniques, some "unaccompanied learning algorithms", "density estimation", among others. In supervised learning, "z = (x, y)" is an instance-label pair, "h" is a predictor, and "f (h; (x, y)) = loss (h (x), y)" is the loss function. In terms of statistical learnability, the goal is to minimize "$F(h) = E_{Z \sim D}[f(h; Z)]$", within experimental accuracy based on finite sample only (z1, ... zm). In this case, care does not concern the computational aspects of the problem, that is to say whether this approximated minimization can be carried out quickly and effectively, but whether this can only be achieved statistically on the basis of the sample (z1,... zm).

It is well known that a "supervised classification and regression" problem can only be learned if the empirical risks for the whole "h ∈ H" are consistent with the population risk. According to the research by Blumer (1989) and Alon (1997), "if uniform convergence applies, then empirical risk minimization (ERM) is consistent, that is, the population risk of the ERM converges to the optimal population risk, and the problem is learnable with the ERM ". This suggests that "uniform convergence" of the empirical risks is a required and satisfactory condition for learnability, which can be depicted as an ambiguity for a "combinatorial state" which, when it comes to classification algorithms, has a finite "VC dimension." when in regression algorithms it has a finite "fat-crushing dimension." The figure below shows a scenario for "controlled classification and regression":

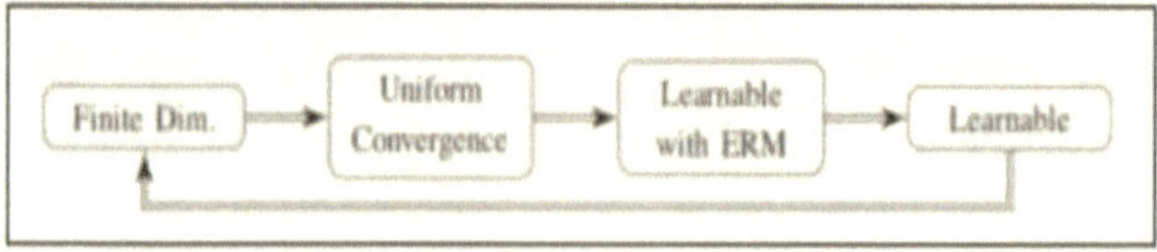

In addition to 'uniform convergence', 'stability' specific concepts were proposed as a learning condition. Inherently, the concepts of "stability" depend on specific "learning laws" or algorithms, and evaluate how sensitive they are to the fluctuations of the training data set. In particular, it is recognized that ERM stability would be sufficient for learnability. It is claimed in "Mukherjee et al. (2006)", that stability is also essential for learning. Assuming that "uniform convergence equates to learnability, stability has been shown to characterize learning skills only when uniform convergence characterizes learning skills".

Only in an environment of "controlled classification and regression" was equivalence of uniform convergence and learning officially established. More generally, the implications for "right" in the above image are valid: "finite fat burning dimensions", "uniform convergence" and even "ERM stability" may be considered suitable for learnability using the "ERM". Regarding the opposite implications, Vapnik has shown that a concept of "non-trivial" or "rigid" learnability related to the ERM is tantamount to "uniform convergence of the empirical risks ". The concept was designed to eliminate some of the "trivial" problems of learning that can be learned without uniform convergence. Even with these problems, empirical risk minimization can make learning feasible. In the 'general learning environment' or 'supervised classification and regression', a problem therefore only seems to be learnable if it can be learned through empirical risk minimization.

This framework is not very specific and can cover a significant part of the widespread optimization and statistical learning difficulties, such as:

Stochastic convex optimization in Hilbert spaces: 'Let' Z 'be any measurable set, let' H 'be a closed, convex and bounded subset of a Hilbert space, and let' f (h; z) 'be Lipschitz continuous and convex wrt his first argument. Here we want to approximately minimize the objective function "Ez~D [f (h; z)]", where the distribution over "Z" is unknown, based on an empirical sample z1, ..., zm ".

Density Estimation: "Let 'Z' be a subset of 'Rn', let 'H' be a series of bounded probability densities at 'Z', and let 'f (h; z) = - log (h (z))'. Here is 'f (•)' just the negative log probability of an instance z according to the hypothesis density 'h' Note that to guarantee the boundary of 'f (•)' we have to assume that 'h (z)' lower is bounded by a positive constant for all 'z ∈ Z' ".

K-Means Clustering in Euclidean Space: "Let Z = Rn, let 'H' be all subsets of Rn of size k, and let 'f (h; z) = minc∈h || c - z || 2'. Here each h represents a series of 'k centroids' and 'f (•)' measures the Euclidean distance squared between an instance z and the nearest center of gravity, according to the hypothesis h ".

Large margin classification in a reproducing kernel Hilbert space (RKHS): "Let 'Z = X × {0,1}', where 'X' is a bounded subset of an RKHS, let 'H' be another bounded subset of the RKHS, and let 'f (h; (x, y)) = max {0, 1 - y⟨x, h⟩}'. Here 'f (•)' is the popular hinge loss function and our goal is to use margin based linear classification to be carried out in the RKHS ".

Regression: "Let 'Z = X × Y' where 'X' and 'Y' are bounded subsets of 'Rn' and 'R' respectively, let 'H' be a series of bounded functions 'h: Xn → R', and let 'f (h; (x, y)) = (h (x) −y) 2'. Here 'f (•)' is simply the squared loss function ".

Binary classification: 'Let' Z = X × {0,1} ', let' H 'be a collection of functions' h: X → {0,1} ', and let' f (h; (x, y)) = 11 {h (x)/= y} '. Here "f (•)" is simply the "0 - 1 loss function", which measures whether the binary hypothesis "h (•)" has misqualified the example (x, y) ".

The ultimate goal of this setting is to select a hypothesis "h ∈ H" based on a finite number of samples with the least potential risk. Overall, we expect sample size to improve the approach to risk. It is believed that "learning guidelines that allow us to choose such hypotheses are consistent." We formally conclude that "line A" is consistent with rate "εcons (m)" under distribution "D" if for all "m", where "F * = infh∈HF (h)", the "rate" ε (m) must be monotonous, decreasing by "εcons (m) - → 0)".

"ES∼Dm [F (A (S)) - F ∗] ≤ εcons (m)"

We cannot choose a "D-based" learning rule because "D" is unknown. Rather, we need a "stronger requirement that the rule be consistent with velocity εcons (m) under all distributions D over Z". The main definition is as follows:

"A learning problem is learnable if there is a learning rule A and a monotonically decreasing $m \to \infty$ series $\varepsilon_{cons}(m)$, so that $\varepsilon_{cons}(m) - \to 0$, and $\forall D$, $E_{S \sim D^m}[F(A(S)) - F*] \leq \varepsilon_{cons}(m)$. A learning rule A to which this applies is referred to as a universally consistent learning rule. "

The above definition of learnability, which requires a uniform rate across all distributions, is the most appropriate concept to study the learnability of a hypothesis class. It is a direct generalization from "agnostic PAC learnability" to "Vapnik's general learning environment" as studied by Haussler in 1992. A potential path to learning is to minimize the empirical risk "FS (h)" over a sample "S", defined as

$$FS(h) = \frac{1}{m} \sum f(h; z)$$

Z, z	"Instance domain and a specific instance."
H, h	"Hypothesis class and a specific hypothesis."
$f(h, z)$	"Loss of hypothesis h on instance z."
B	"$\sup_{h,z} \lvert f(h; z) \rvert$"
D	"Underlying distribution on instance domain Z"
S	"Empirical sample $z1, \ldots, zm$, sampled i.i.d. from D"
m	"Size of empirical sample S"
$A(S)$	"Learning rule A applied to empirical sample S"
$\varepsilon_{cons}(m)$	"Rate of consistency for a learning rule"
$F(h)$	"Risk of hypothesis h, $E_{z \sim D}[f(h; z)]$"
$F*$	"$\inf_{h \in H} F(h)$"
$FS(h)$	"Empirical risk of hypothesis h on sample S, $\frac{1}{m}\sum_{z \in S} f(h; z)$"
$\hat{h}_S$	"An ERM hypothesis, $FS(\hat{h}_S) = \inf_{h \in H} FS(h)$"
$\varepsilon_{erm}(m)$	"Rate of AERM for a learning rule"
$\varepsilon_{stable}(m)$	"Rate of stability for a learning rule"
$\varepsilon_{gen}(m)$	"Rate of generalization for a learning rule"

The 'rule A' is an 'Empirical risk minimization' if it can minimize the empirical risk

$$FS(A(S)) = FS(\hat{h}_S) = \inf_{h \in H} FS(h)$$

where "FS (h^S) = infh∈H FS (h)" is referred to as the "minimum empirical risk". Given the probability that multiple hypotheses minimize the empirical risk, "h^S" does not relate to a particular hypothesis and there may be multiple lines all of which are "ERM".

"Rule A" can therefore be considered as an "AERM (Asymptotic Empirical Risk Minimizer) with velocity εerm (m) under distribution D" when:

"ES~Dm [FS (A (S)) - FS (h^S)] ≤ εerm (m)"

A learning rule can be considered an "AERM universal" with "rate εerm (m)" if it is an AERM with "rate εerm (m)" under all distributions "D" over "Z". A learning rule can be considered "always AERM" with "rate εerm (m)", if for an "S" sample the size is "FS (A (S)) - FS (h^S) ≤ εerm (m) ".

It can be concluded that "rule A" generalizes with rate "εgen (m)" under distribution D if for all m, where A rule "universally generalizes with rate εgen (m) if it generalizes with rate εgen (m) among all distributions D over Z ".

"ES~Dm [| F (A (S)) - FS (A (S)) |] ≤ εgen (m)"

Impact of uniform convergence on learnability

Uniform convergence is considered to apply to learning difficulties, 'if the empirical risks of hypotheses in the hypothesis class converge uniformly with their population risk, with a distribution-independent rate':

"Sup D ES~Dm [suph∈H | F (h) −FS (h) |] - m → ∞ → 0"

It is easy to demonstrate that a problem can be considered learnable using the "ERM learning rule" as uniform convergence.

In 1971, Chervonenkis and Vapnik showed that 'the finitude of an uncomplicated combinatorial measure known as the VC dimension indicates uniform convergence, for binary classification problems (where $Z = X \times \{0, 1\}$, each hypothesis is a mapping of X to $\{0, 1\}$ and $f(h; (x, y)) = 1\{h(x) /= y\})$ '. It can also be confirmed that problems related to binary classification in infinite "VC dimension" cannot be learned in a distribution independent sense. As a necessary and sufficient condition for learning, this identifies the situation of having a finite "VC dimension", and thus uniform convergence.
This characterization is also extensible for "regression" techniques, namely "squared loss regression, where h is now a truly valued function, and $f(h; (x, y)) = (h(x) - y)2$" The property of having a "finite fat-burning dimension" on all finite scales can replace the property of containing "finite VC dimensions", but the basic equivalence still contains a problem that can only be learned if there is uniform convergence These findings are generally based on sensible reductions made to binary classification, although the perceived "general learning environment" is not as specific as classification and regression, including scenarios in which it is difficult to reduce classification to binary classification.

In 1998, Vapnik attempted to portray that "in the general learning environment, learnability with the ERM learning rule is equivalent to uniform convergence", to reinforce the need for uniform convergence in this setting, noting that the result may not be true for "trivial" Situations. In particular, cases related to "random learning problem with hypothesis class H and H add to a single hypothesis h̃ such that f (h̃, z) <inf h∈H f (h, z) for all z ∈ Z "as shown in the figure below. This particular learning problem can be" trivially "learned using the" ERM learning rule "which always chooses" hh ". Although" H "can be any complex without prior assumptions and uniform convergence It should be noted that this does not apply to binary classification models, where "f (h; (x, y)) = 11 {h (x)/= y}", since "(x, y)" there will be hypotheses with "f (h; (x, y)) = f (h̃; (x, y))" therefore, if "H" is very complex with infinite "VC dimensions, then multiple hypotheses will have" 0 "Empirical error on a given training data set.

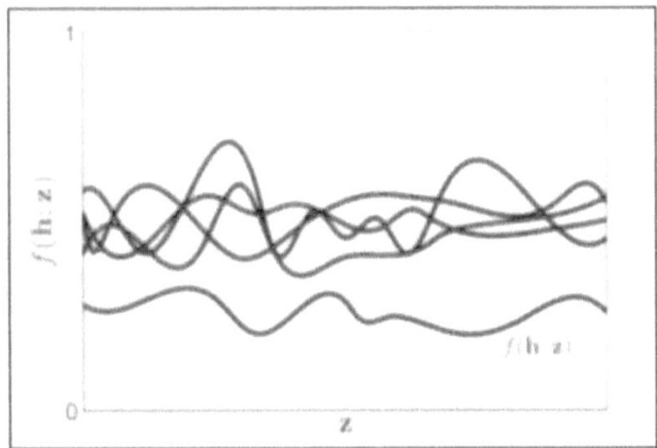

To remove such a "trivial" scenario, Vapnik proposed the concept of "strict consistency" as an even stronger version of consistency. It is defined by the equation below, where the convergence is within the probability.

"∀c ∈ R, inf h: F (h) ≥c FS (h) - m → ∞ → inf h: F (h) ≥c F (h)"

The idea is that the empirical risk of "ERM" is essential for least potential risk convergence, even if the "good" hypotheses with less risk than the threshold are removed. Vapnik has succeeded in proving that such "strict consistency" of the ERM is essentially equivalent to uniform convergence, probably in form. The equivalence below applies to each individual distribution and is independent of the universal consistency of the "Empirical Risk Minimizer".

"Sup h∈H (F (h) - FS (h)) - m → ∞ → 0"

On the basis of this research it can be implied that "up to trivial situations a uniform convergence property indeed characterizes learnability, at least using the ERM learning rule".

Learnability without uniform convergence

A 'stochastic convex optimization' or learnability without a uniform convergence problem can be considered an exceptional case of the 'general learning environment' explained above, including additional limitations that 'the objective function f (h; z) is lipschitz continuous and convex in hfor every z, and that H is closed, convex and bounded ". The problems where "H" is a subset of a "Hilbert space" will be addressed here. An exceptional scenario is "the well-known linear prediction setting, where z = (x, y) is an instance-label pair, each hypothesis h belongs to a subset H of a Hilbert space, and f (h; x, y) = 1 (⟨H , φ (x)⟩, y) for some feature mapping φ and a loss function l: R × Y → R, which is convex with respect to the first argument ".

The scenario has been successfully established with the stochastic dependence of "h" being linear, similar to the previous example, has been successfully established. When the "domain H" and "image φ" are bounded, there is uniform convergence, which means that " | F (h) - FS (h) | " is uniformly bounded in general "h ∈ H". This uniform convergence from "FS (h) to F (h)" validates the selection of the empirical minimizer "h^S = arg minhFS (h)" and causes the expected value of "F (h^S)" to converge to the optimal value "F ∗ = inf hF (h)".

Although the dependence on "h" is non-linear, uniform convergence can still be determined using "overlay number arguments" provided that "H" is a finite dimension. Unfortunately, it is possible that there is no uniform convergence when we move to the infinite-dimensional hypothesis and empirical minimization may not allow the algorithm to learn. Notably, this does not mean that the problem can be considered "unlearnable". It can be shown that even if uniform convergence does not exist, regularization mechanisms can develop a learning algorithm to solve any problem with "stochastic convex optimization". This mechanism is directly related to the principle of stability. For example, let's look at the 'convex stochastic optimization' problem given by the equation in the figure below, where for this example 'H' the 'd-dimensional unit sphere H = hRd: | h | ≤1 "," z = (x, α) with α ∈ [0, 1] d "and" x ∈ H ", and" u ∗ v "can be defined as an element-by-product.

$$f^{(3)}(h;(x,\alpha)) \;=\; \|\alpha * (h - x)\| \;=\; \sqrt{\sum_i \alpha^2[i](h[i] - x[i])^2}$$

Now consider a series of learning difficulties, where "d = 2m" for each sample size "m", and note that a "convergence rate independent of the dimensionality" d "is not to be expected. This matter can be formalized into infinite dimensions The learning problem in the above equation can be considered "that of finding the center of an unknown distribution over x ∈ Rd, where stochastic confidence measurements per coordinate" α [i] "are also available." For now, we focus on the scenario where certain coordinates are missing, meaning "α [i] = 0".
By taking into account the distribution below over "(x, α): x = 0" with probability as 1, and "α" is uniform over "{0, 1} d". That is, "α [i]" are independent and identically distributed uniform "Bernoulli". For a random sample "(x1, α1), ..., (xm, αm)" if "d> 2m" then that is a result of probability greater than "1 - e - 1> 0.63" and a coordinate "j ∈ 1... d" is such that all "confidence vectors αi" in the sample are "0" at the coordinate "j", ie "αi [j] = 0" for all "i = 1 .. m ". Suppose that" ej ∈ H "is the" standard vector corresponding to this coordinate. "Then, in the equation in the figure below," FS (3) (•) "represents the empirical risk related to the function" f (3) (•) ".

$$F_S^{(3)}(\mathbf{e}_j) \;=\; \frac{1}{m}\sum_{i=1}^{m}\left\|\alpha_i * (\mathbf{e}_j - 0)\right\| \;=\; \frac{1}{m}\sum_{i=1}^{m}|\alpha_i[j]| \;=\; 0$$

In another scenario, if "FS (3) (•)" indicates the actual risk to the function "f (3) (•)", the equation in the figure below is obtained.

$$F^{(3)}(\mathbf{e}_j) \;=\; \mathbb{E}_{\mathbf{x},\alpha}\left[\left\|\alpha * (\mathbf{e}_j - 0)\right\|\right] \;=\; \mathbb{E}_{\mathbf{x},\alpha}\left[\|\alpha[j]\|\right] \;=\; 1/2$$

So for each sample size "m", a convex "Lipschitz continuous objective" can be constructed in a dimension high enough to ensure that with a minimum "0.63 probability" over the sample, "suph | F (3) (h) −F (3) (h) | ≥ ½ ". Since" f (•; •) "is non-negative," ej "may additionally be referred to as an" empirical minimizer ", although the expected value is" F (3) (ej) = ½ "not at all close to the optimal expected value" minhF (3) (h) = F (3) (0) = 0 ".

To explain this case with an approach that does not depend on the sample size, suppose "H is the unit sphere of an infinite dimensional Hilbert space with orthonormal base e1, e2, ..., where for v ∈ H we refer to its coordinates v [j] = <v, ej> "with respect to its base". The "confidences α" serve as a map of each individual coordinate to "[0, 1]". This means an "infinite series of reals in [0, 1]". The operation of the product according to the elements, "α ∗ v" is defined based on this image and the objective function "f (3) (•)" of the equation (shown in the first image of this example) can be easily defined can be in this infinite-dimensional space.

Now let's rethink the distribution over "z = (x, α)", where "x = 0" and "α" is an infinitely independent and identically distributed set of "uniform Bernoulli random variables" (ie a "Bernoulli process with any αi uniform more than {0, 1} and independent of all other αj "). It can be implied that for every finite sample there is a high probability of finding a coordinate" j "with" αi [j] = 0 "for all" I ", and therefore an empirical minimizer" FS (3) (ej) = 0 "with" F (3) (ej) = 1/2> 0 = F (3) (0) "can be obtained.

Accordingly, it can be noted that the empirical values "FS (3) (h)" are not uniform as they converge as expected, and empirical minimization does not guarantee a solution to the learning problem. Moreover, one could potentially generate a sharper counterexample, where the "unique empirical minimizer h^S" is nowhere near the optimal expected value. To achieve this, "f (3) (•)" needs to be supplemented by using "a small term that makes the empirical minimizer unique and not too close to the origin". Considering the equation below where "$\varepsilon = 0.01$".

"F (4) (h; (x, α)) = f (3) (h; (x, α)) + $\varepsilon\sum 2$ - i (h [i] −1) 2"

The target remains convex and "(1 + ε)" is still "Lipschitz". Since the added term is strictly convex, the "f (4) (h; z)" will also be strictly convex with respect to "h" and that is why the empirical minimizer is unique.

Considering the same distribution over "z: x = 0" while "α [i]" are independent and uniformly distributed uniformly 0 or 1. The minimizer of "FS (4) (h)" is called the empirical minimizer subject to the constraints "| h | ≤ 1". The good news is that while identifying the solution for such a limited optimization problem is complicated, it is not mandatory. Suffice it to say that "the optimum of the unlimited optimization problem h ∗ UC = arg minFS (4) (h) (without limitation h ∈ H) norm | h ∗ UC | ≥ 1 ".

It should be noted that "in the unlimited problem, where αi [j] = 0 for all i = 1 … n, only the second term of f (4) depends on h [j] and we have h * UC [j] = 1 "Since it can happen for certain coordinates" j ", it can be concluded that" the solution to the limited optimization problem is on the boundary of H, ie | h^ S | = 1 ", which can be represented by the equation in the

$$F^{*}(\hat{h}_S) \geq E_{\alpha}\left[\sqrt{\sum_i \alpha_i \hat{h}_S^2(i)}\right] \geq E_{\alpha}\left[\sum_i \alpha_i \hat{h}_S^2(i)\right] = \sum_i \hat{h}_S^2(i) E_{\alpha}(\alpha_i) = \frac{1}{2}\|\hat{h}_S\|^2 = \frac{1}{2}$$

picture below while" F $*$ ≤ F (0) = ε ".

Chapter 6 : Data Science Lifecycle and Technologies

The earliest recorded use of the term data science dates back to 1960 and is attributed to "Peter Naur", who reportedly used the term data science as a substitute for computer science and eventually introduced the term "data logy". In 1974 Naur released his book entitled "Concise Survey of Computer Methods", which used the term data science liberally throughout the book. In 1992, the contemporary definition of data science was presented at "The Second Japanese-French Statistics Symposium", recognizing the emergence of a new discipline that focuses primarily on data types, dimensions and structures.

The term Data can be defined as "information processed and stored by a computer". Our digital world has flooded our reality with data. From a click on a website to our smartphones that track and record our location every second of the day, our world is drowning in the data. From the depth of this gigantic data, solutions to our problems that we have not even encountered can be extracted. This particular process of collecting insights from a measurable set of data using mathematical equations and statistics can be defined as "data science". The role of data scientists is often very versatile and is often confused with a computer scientist and a statistician. Essentially, anyone, whether a person or a company, who wants to dig deep into large amounts of data to collect information, can be referred to us as a data scientist. For example, companies such as "Amazon" and "Target" track and record in-store and online purchases made by customers to provide personalized recommendations for products and services. The social media platforms, such as "Twitter" and "Instagram", which allow users to identify their current location, can identify global migration patterns by analyzing the wealth of data that users themselves receive.

Data science life cycle

The most recommended lifecycle for structured data science projects is the "Team Data Science Process" (TDSP). This process is widely used for projects where applications need to be implemented based on artificial intelligence and / or machine learning algorithms. It can also be adapted for and used in the implementation of "exploratory data science" projects and "ad hoc analytics" projects. The TDSP lifecycle is designed as a nimble and sequential iteration of steps that guide the tasks required to use predictive models. These predictive models must be deployed in the company's production environment so that they can be used in the development of basic artificial intelligence applications. The purpose of this data science lifecycle is the rapid delivery and completion of a data science project to a defined engagement endpoint. Seamless execution of any data science project requires effective communication of tasks within the team and to stakeholders.

The fundamental components of the "Team Data Science Process" are:

Definition of a data science life cycle

The five main stages of the TDSP lifecycle that outline the interactive steps required to implement the project from start to finish are: "Business Insight", "Understanding Data Acquisition", "Modeling", "Implementation" and " customer acceptance ". Keep reading to learn more about this soon!

Standardized project structure

To enable seamless and easy access to project documents for team members for quick information retrieval, the use of templates and a shared directory structure goes a long way. All project documents and the project code our shop and a "version management system" such as "TFS", "Git" or "Subversion" for improved team collaboration. Business requirements and associated tasks and functionalities are stored in a flexible project tracking system such as "JIRA", "Rally" and "Azure DevOps" to enable improved code tracking for each individual functionality. These tools also help estimate the resources and costs involved throughout the project lifecycle. To ensure effective management of each project, information security, and team collaboration, TDSP grants the creation of separate storage for each project on the version management system Adopting a standardized structure for all projects within an organization, helps to create institutional knowledge library throughout the organization.

The TDSP lifecycle provides standard templates for all required documents and the folder structure in a central location. The programming code files for the data exploration and extraction of the functionality can be organized using the supplied folder structure, which also contains records of model iterations. With these templates, team members can easily understand the work completed by others and new team members can be seamlessly added to a particular project. The markdown format supports accessibility as well as editing or updating the document templates. In order to ensure that the goal and objectives of the project are well defined and also to guarantee the expected quality of the products to be delivered, these templates contain various checklists with important questions for each project. For example, a "project charter" can be used to document the project size and business problem that the project solves; standardized data reports are used to document the "structure and statistics" of the data.

Infrastructure and resources for data science projects

To effectively store the infrastructure and manage shared analytics, the TDSP recommends using tools such as: machine learning service, databases, big data clusters, and cloud-based systems to store datasets. The analysis and storage infrastructure that houses raw as well as processed or cleaned data sets can be cloud-based or on-premises. D Analysis and Storage Infrastructure enables reproducibility of analysis and prevents duplication and redundancy of data that can cause inconsistency and unjustified infrastructure costs. Tools are provided to grant specific permissions to the shared resources and to track their activity, which in turn allows secure access to the resources for each team member.

Project execution tools and utilities

Making changes to an existing process is quite challenging in most organizations. To encourage and increase the consistency of approval of these changes, various tools provided by the TDSP can be implemented. Some of the basic lifecycle tasks of data science, including "data exploration" and "basic modeling", can be easily automated with the tools provided by TDSP. To enable the hassle-free contribution of shared tools and utilities to the team's shared code repository, TDSP offers a well-defined structure. This results in cost savings because other project teams within the organization can reuse and reuse these shared tools and utilities.

The TDSP lifecycle serves as a standardized template with a well-defined set of artifacts that can be used to achieve effective team collaboration and communication across the board. This lifecycle consists of a selection of "Microsoft" best practices and structures to enable successful delivery of predictive analytics solutions and intelligent applications.

Let's take a look at the details of each of the five stages of the TDSP lifecycle, namely 'business understanding',

'understanding data acquisition', 'modeling', 'implementation' and 'customer acceptance'.

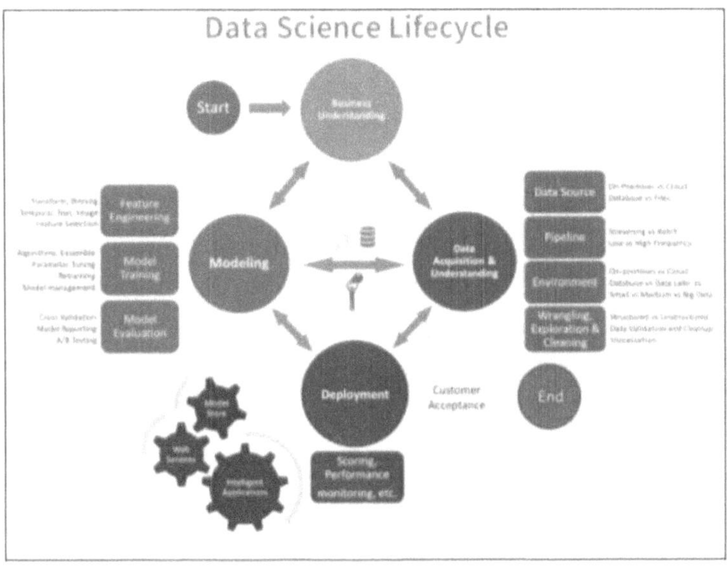

Phase I - Business understanding

The aim of this phase is to collect and go deeper into the essential variables that will be used as targets for the model, and the metrics associated with these variables will ultimately determine the overall success of the project. Another important objective of this phase is to identify the required data sources that the company already has or may need to purchase. At this stage, the two main tasks to be performed are "defining objects and identifying data sources".

Products to be delivered in this phase

• Charter Document - It is a "living document" that needs to be updated throughout the project to reflect new project discoveries and evolving business requirements. A standard template is included with the TDSP "Project Structure Definition". It is important to build on this document by adding more details as the project progresses, while keeping stakeholders quickly informed of any changes made.
• Data Sources - In the TDSP "Project Data Reports Folder", the data sources can be found in the "Raw Data Sources" section of the "Data Definitions Report". The "Raw Data Sources" section also specifies the start and end locations of the raw data and provides additional details such as the "encoding scripts" to move the data into any environment.
• Data dictionaries - The descriptions of the characteristics and characteristics of the data, such as the "data schemes" and available "entity relationship schemes", provided by the stakeholders, are documented in the data dictionaries.

Phase II - Data acquisition and understanding

The aim of this phase is to produce high-quality processed
dataset with defined relationships to the model goals and
location of the dataset in the required analysis environment.
At this stage, the "data architecture" solution architecture
should also be developed which will allow for regular updates
and scoring of the data. The three main tasks to be carried out
at this stage are: "Data recording, data exploration and data
pipeline set up".

Data recording

The process required to transfer the data from the source
location to the target location should be initiated at this stage.
The target locations are determined by the environments in
which you can perform analytical activities, such as training
and predictions.

Data exploration

The data set must be removed to remove any discrepancies and errors before it can be used to train the data models. To control the data quality and collected information required to process the data before modeling it, tools such as data summary and visualization should be used. Since this process is repeated several times, an automated utility called "IDEAR", provided by TDSP, can be used for data visualization and data summary report creation. With the attainment of a satisfactory quality of the processed data, the inherent data patterns can be observed. This, in turn, aids in the selection and development of an appropriate "predictive model" for the target. Now you need to assess whether you have the required amount of data to start the modeling process, which is iterative and may require you to identify new data sources to achieve higher relevance and accuracy.

Set up a data pipeline

To complement the iterative data modeling process, a standard process for scoring new data and renewing the existing data set should be established by setting up a "data pipeline or workflow". The data pipeline solution architecture should be developed by the end of this phase. There are three types of pipelines that can be used based on the business needs and limitations of the existing system: "batch-based", "real-time or streaming" and "hybrid".

Products to be delivered in this phase

• Data Quality Report - This report should include "data summary", the relationship between business need and characteristics, and variable rankings. The "IDEAR" tool included with TDSP is capable of generating data quality reports on a relational table, CSV file or other tabular data set.
• Solution Architecture - A description or diagram of the data pipeline used to score new data and generate predictions after the model is built can be referred to as "solution architecture". This diagram can also provide a data pipeline needed to "retrain" the model based on new data.
• Checkpoint decision - Before starting the actual model building process, the project must be re-evaluated to determine whether the expected value can be achieved by continuing the project. These are also referred to as "Go or No-Go" decisions.

Stage III - Modeling

The aim of this phase is to find "optimal data attributes" for the machine learning model, which is informative enough to accurately predict the target variables and can be deployed in the production environment. The three main tasks to be fulfilled in this phase are: "feature engineering, model training and determining the suitability of the model for the production environment".

Products to be delivered in this phase

• Feature Sets - The document that contains all the features described in the "Feature Sets of the Data Definition Report" section. It is widely used by the programmers to write the required code and develop functions based on a description in the document.
• Model Report - This document must include the details of each model that has been evaluated based on a standard template report.
• Checkpoint decisions - A decision on the implementation of the model in the production environment must be made based on the performance of different models.

Stage IV implementation

The goal of this phase is to release the solution models to a lower production-like environment, such as a pre-production environment and a user acceptance test environment, before finally implementing the model in the production environment. The primary task to be fulfilled at this stage is "operationalization of the model".

Operationalize the model

Once you have obtained a set of models with expected levels of performance, these models can then be operationalized to use other applicable applications. Depending on the business requirements, predictions can be made in real time or on a batch basis. In order to implement the model, they must be integrated with an open "Application Programming Interface" (API) to allow interaction of the model with all other applications and its components, if necessary.

Products to be delivered in this phase

• A dashboard report with key performance indicators and metrics to access the health of the system.
• Run a document or book detailing the implementation plan for the final model.
• A document with the solution architecture of the final model.

Phase V - Customer acceptance

The purpose of this phase is to ensure that the final solution for the project meets stakeholders' expectations and meets the business requirements gathered during Phase I of the Data Science lifecycle. The two main tasks to be performed at this stage are: "system validation and project transfer".

Products to be delivered in this phase

The main document created at this stage is for stakeholders and is referred to as an 'exit report'. The document contains all available details of the project which are important to provide insight into the operation of the system. TDSP provides a standardized "exit report" template that can be easily adapted to the specific needs of stakeholders.

Importance of Data Science

The ability to analyze and accurately investigate data trends and patterns using machine learning algorithms has resulted in the significant application of data science in the cybersecurity space. Using data science, companies are not only able to identify the specific network terminal (s) that initiated the cyber attack, but they are also able to predict potential future attacks on their systems and take the necessary measures to attack them. in the first place. The use of "active intrusion detection systems" capable of monitoring users and devices on any network and flagging unusual activities serves as a powerful weapon against hackers and cyber attackers. While the
"Predictive Intrusion Detection Systems" that can use machine learning algorithms on historical data to detect potential security threats serve as a powerful shield against cyber predators.

Cyber attacks can lead to the loss of invaluable data and information, which can lead to extreme damage to the organization. To secure and protect the data set, advanced encryption and complex signatures can be used to prevent unauthorized access. Data science can help develop such impenetrable protocols and algorithms. By analyzing the trends and patterns of previous cyber attacks on companies in different industrial sectors, Data Science can help detect the most targeted data set and even predict potential future cyber attacks. Businesses rely heavily on data generated and authorized by their customers, but in the face of increasing cyber attacks, customers are extremely wary of compromising their personal information and want to take their businesses to the companies that give them ensure their data security and privacy by implementing advanced data security tools and technologies. This is where data science becomes the saving grace of the companies by helping them improve their cybersecurity measures.

Data science has enabled the use of advanced machine learning algorithms that have a wide variety of applications across multiple industrial domains. For example, the development of self-driving cars that are able to collect real-time data using their advanced cameras and sensors to map their surroundings and make decisions about vehicle speed and other driving maneuvers. Companies are always on the hunt to better understand their customers' needs. This is now achievable by gathering data from existing sources such as customer order history, recently viewed items, gender, age and demographics, and applying advanced analytical tools and algorithms to this data to gain valuable insights. Using ML algorithms, the system can generate product recommendations for individual customers with greater accuracy. The smart consumer is always looking for the most engaging and enhanced user experience so that companies can use these analytical tools and algorithms to gain a competitive advantage and grow their business.

Data science strategies

Data science is primarily used in decision making by making accurate predictions using predictive causal analytics, prescriptive analytics and machine learning.
Predictive causal analysis - The 'predictive causal analysis' can be used to develop a model that can accurately predict and predict the probability of a particular event in the future. For example, financial institutions use predictive causal analysis tools to assess the likelihood of a customer defaulting on their credit card payments by generating a model that can analyze the customer's payment history with all their lending institutions.

Prescriptive analytics - The 'prescriptive analytics' are widely used in the development of 'intelligent tools and applications' capable of modifying and learning with dynamic parameters and making their own 'decisions'. The tool not only predicts the occurrence of a future event, but can also make recommendations for different actions and the resulting results. For example, the self-driving cars collect driving-related data with each driving experience and use it to train themselves to make better driving and maneuvering decisions.

Machine learning to make predictions - To develop models that can determine future trends based on the transaction data the company has collected, machine learning algorithms are a necessity. This is considered to be under the supervision of machine learning, which we will discuss later in this book. For example, fraud detection systems use machine learning algorithms on the historical fraudulent purchase data to detect if a transaction is fraudulent.

Machine learning for pattern discovery - In order to develop models that are able to identify hidden data patterns, but lack the required parameters to make future predictions, the 'unaccompanied machine learning algorithms' such as 'Clustering' must be used . For example, telecom companies often use "clustering" technology to expand their network by identifying network tower locations with optimal signal strength in the targeted region.

Artificial intelligence

Humans or Homo Sapiens often call themselves the most superior species to ever have housed planet Earth, attributing them primarily to their "intelligence." Even the most complex animal behavior is never considered intelligent, but the simplest of human behavior is attributed to intelligence. For example, if a female digger wasp returns with food to her burrow, she puts the food on the doorstep and checks for intruders before carrying her food inside. Sounds like an intelligent wasp, right? But an experiment with these wasps, in which the scientist moved the food not too far from the entrance to the burrow while the wasp was in it, revealed that the wasps continued to repeat the entire procedure every time the food was moved from its original location. This experiment concluded that the wasp's inability to adapt to changing conditions and therefore "intelligence" is noticeably absent in the wasps. So what is this "human intelligence"? Psychologists characterize human intelligence as a composite of multiple skills, such as learning from experiences and adapting to them, understanding abstract concepts, reasoning, problem solving, language use and perception.
The science of developing human-controlled and operated machines, such as digital computers or robots, that can mimic human intelligence, adapt to new inputs and perform tasks such as humans, is called "artificial intelligence" (AI). Thanks to Hollywood, most people think that robots come to life and wreak havoc on the planet when they hear the words artificial intelligence. But that is far from the truth. The core principle of artificial intelligence is the ability of the AI-powered machines to rationalize (think like people) and take actions (mimic human actions) to achieve the intended goal. Easy said,

Artificial intelligence is the creation of a machine that will think and act as people. The three main goals of artificial intelligence are learning, reasoning and perception.

Although the term artificial intelligence was coined in 1956, the British computer science pioneer Alan Mathison Turing pioneered artificial intelligence in the mid-20th century. In 1935, Turing developed an abstract calculator with a scanner and unlimited memory in the form of symbols. The scanner was able to move back and forth through the memory, read the existing symbols and write further symbols from the memory. A programming instruction would dictate the actions of the scanner and also be stored in memory. For example, Turing generated a machine with implicit learning capabilities that could change and improve programming. This concept is commonly known as the universal "Turing Machine" and serves as the basis for all modern computers. Turing claimed that computers could learn from their own experience and solve problems using a guiding principle known as "heuristic problem solving".

In the 1950s, early AI research focused on problem solving and symbolic methods. By the 1960s, AI research had taken a leap forward from "The US Department of Defense," which began to train computers to mirror human reasoning. In the 1970s, the Defense Advanced Research Projects Agency (DARPA) successfully completed street mapping projects. You may be surprised to learn that DARPA produced intelligent personal assistants in 2003, long before the famous Siri and Alexa existed. Obviously, this groundbreaking work in the field of AI has paved the way for automation and reasoning observed in modern computers.

These are the main human traits we want to emulate in the machines:

Knowledge - In order for machines to act and act like people, they need an abundance of data and information from the world around us. To implement knowledge technology, AI must have seamless access to data objects, data categories, and data properties, as well as the relationship between them that can be managed and stored in the data store.

Learning - Of all the different forms of learning that apply to AI, the simplest method is trial and error. For example, a chess learning computer program will try all possible moves until the mat-in-one move is found to end the game. This move is then stored by the program to be used the next time it encounters the same position. This relatively easy-to-implement aspect of learning, called "rote learning," involves easy remembering of individual items and procedures. The most challenging part of learning is called "generalization," which means that past experience is applied to the associated new scenarios.

Troubleshooting - The systematic process of achieving a predefined goal or solution by searching a range of possible actions can be defined as troubleshooting. The problem solving techniques can be adapted for a particular problem or used for a wide variety of problems. A common problem solving method commonly used in AI is "resource-end analysis", which subtracts the difference between the current state and the final state of the target in steps. Think about some of the basic functions of a robot, moving back and forth or picking up things that lead to a goal being fulfilled.

Reasoning - Reasoning can be defined as the ability to make inferences appropriate to the given situation. The two forms of reasoning are called "deductive reasoning" and "inductive reasoning." According to "deductive reasoning," it is believed that if the premise is true, the conclusion is true. On the other hand, in the "inductive reasoning", even if the premise is true, the conclusion may or may not be true. While considerable success has been achieved in programming computers to perform deductive reasoning, the implementation of "true reasoning" remains aloof and one of the greatest challenges that artificial intelligence faces.

Perception - The process of generating a multidimensional image of an object using different sensory organs can be defined as perception. This creation of environmental awareness is complicated by several factors, such as the viewing angle, the direction and intensity of the light, and the amount of contrast the object produces with the surrounding field. Breakthrough developments have been made in the field of artificial perception and can be easily observed in our daily lives with the advent of self-driving cars and robots that can collect empty soda cans as they move through the buildings.

Chapter 7 : Business Intelligence vs. Data Science

Data science as you have learned by now is an interdisciplinary approach that applies mathematical algorithms and statistical tools to extract valuable insights from raw data. On the other hand, Business Intelligence (BI) refers to the application of analytical tools and technologies to gain a deeper understanding of the current state of the company in relation to the historical performance of the company. Simply put, BI provides the company with intelligence by analyzing their current and historical data, while data science is much more powerful and capable of analyzing the massive volume of raw data to make future predictions.

An avalanche of qualitative and quantitative data coming in from a wide variety of input sources has created a dependence on data science for companies to understand and use this data to maintain and expand their businesses. The emergence of data science as the ultimate decision-making tool shows the increasing data dependence for companies. In some cases, Business Intelligence tasks may be automated using data science tools and technologies. The ability to collect insights from the Internet using these automated tools around the world will only encourage the use of "centralized repositories" for ordinary business users.

Business intelligence is traditionally used for "descriptive analysis" and provides companies with wisdom afterwards. On the other hand, data science is much more futuristic and is used for "predictive and prescriptive analysis". While data science tries to answer questions like "Why did the event happen and could it happen again in the future?", Business Intelligence focuses on questions like "What happened during the event and what can be changed to solve it ? ". It is this fundamental distinction between the "W's" addressed by each of these two fields that sets them apart.

The business intelligence niche was once dominated by technology users with IT expertise, but data science is renewing the business intelligence space by allowing non-technical and core business users to perform analytics and BI activities. Once the data is operationalized by the data scientists, the tools are easy to use for the common business corridor and can be easily maintained by a support team, without the need for any data science expertise. Business intelligence experts are increasingly working hand in hand with the data scientist to develop the best possible data models and solutions for businesses.

Unlike Business Intelligence which is used to create data reports, mainly performance indicators and metric dashboards, and to provide supporting information for the data management strategy, Data Science is used to create forecasts and forecasts using advanced tools and statistics and to provide additional information for data management. A major difference between data science and business intelligence lies in the scope and scale of "built-in machine learning libraries", which enable the everyday business user to perform semi-automated or automated data analysis activities. Consider data science as steroid business intelligence that will turn the world of business analysis into a democracy!

Data mining

Data mining can be defined as "the process of exploring and analyzing large amounts of data to gather meaningful patterns and rules." Data mining falls under the umbrella of data science and is widely used to build artificial intelligence based machine learning models, for example search engine algorithms. Although the process of "digging through data" to discover hidden patterns and predict future events has long been called "knowledge discovery in databases," the term "data mining" was first coined in the 1990s.

According to SAS, "only unstructured data makes up 90% of the digital universe." This avalanche of big data would not essentially guarantee more knowledge. The application of data mining technology makes it possible to filter all redundant and unnecessary data noise in order to gain insight into relevant information that can be used in the immediate decision-making process.

Data mining consists of three fundamental and closely intertwined scientific disciplines, namely "statistics" (the mathematical study of data relationships), "machine learning algorithms" (algorithms that can be trained with an inherent learning ability) and "artificial intelligence" (machines that human-like intelligence). With the advent of big data, data mining technology has been developed to keep up with the 'limitless potential of big data' and relatively cheaper advanced computing capabilities. The once-tedious, labor-intensive and time-consuming activities are automated using advanced processing speed and power of modern computer systems.

Data Mining Trends

Increased computer speed

With the increasing volume and complexity of big data, data mining tools need more powerful and faster computers to analyze data efficiently. Existing statistical techniques such as "clustering" art equipment to process only thousands of input data with a limited number of variables. However, companies are collecting over millions of new data observations with hundreds of variables, making the analysis too complicated to be processed by the computer system. Big data will continue to explode, demanding supercomputers powerful enough to analyze growing big data quickly and efficiently.

Language standardization

The data science community is actively seeking to standardize a language for the data mining process. This ongoing effort allows an analyst to easily work with different data mining platforms by mastering one standard data mining language.

Scientific mining

The success of data mining technology in the industrial world has caught the attention of the scientific and academic research community. For example, psychologists use 'association analysis' to record hair and identify human behavioral patterns for research purposes. Economists use protective analysis algorithms to predict future market trends by analyzing current market variables.

Web mining

Web mining is "the process of discovering hidden data patterns and chains using comparable data mining techniques and applying them directly on the Internet." The 3 main types of web mining are: "content mining", "usage mining" and "structure mining". For example, Amazon uses web mining to understand customer interactions with their website and mobile application to provide their customers with a more engaging and enhanced user experience.

Data Mining Tools

Some of the most commonly used tools for data mining are:

Orange
Orange is "open-source component-based software written in Python". It is most commonly used for basic data mining analysis and offers advanced data processing functions.

RapidMiner

RapidMiner is "open-source component-based software written in Java". It is most commonly used for "predictive analysis" and provides integrated environments for "machine learning", "deep learning" and "text mining".

Mahout

Mahout is an open source platform mainly used for unattended learning process "and developed by" Apache ". It is most commonly used to develop "machine learning algorithms for clustering, classification and joint filtering". This software requires advanced knowledge and expertise to take full advantage of the platform.

MicroStrategy

MicroStrategy is a "business intelligence and data analysis software that can complement all data mining models". This platform offers a variety of drivers and gateways to seamlessly connect to any business resource and analyze complex big data by converting it into accessible visualisations that can be easily shared across the organization.

Conclusion

Thank you for reaching the end of Machine Learning Mathematics: Study Deep Learning through Data Science. How to build artificial intelligence through concepts of statistics, algorithms, analysis and data mining. Let's hope it was informative and could provide you with all the tools you need to achieve your goals, whatever they are.

The next step is to make the most of your newfound wisdom on the mathematical or statistical workings of machine learning technology. The fourth industrial revolution would change the world as we know it today with machines now used by people in limited capacity in a utopian world of science fiction films, where machines are indistinguishable from humans. This transition was made possible with the power of machine learning.

You now have an understanding of the statistical learning framework and the crucial role that uniform convergence and finite classes play in determining whether a problem can be solved with machine learning. To truly capture the essence of machine learning development, expert knowledge and understanding of the underlying statistical framework can mean the difference between a successful machine learning model and a failed model that is a machine that costs time and money.

To become an expert in machine learning, a good understanding of the statistical and mathematical concepts of this field is just as important as learning the required programming language. This may seem daunting to most beginners, but with this book we have provided a simplified explanation of the statistical learning framework for better understanding. A primary requirement for the development of a winning machine learning algorithm is the quality and generation of the required training data set and its learnability by the algorithm. This is why we explained the nuances of training Neural Network in explicit detail by building data from the beginning of the project to the implementation and scoring of the model, along with different types of approached Neural Network training. With this knowledge, you are all equipped to design the required machine learning algorithms for your business needs. If you are a software developer looking for that next great application that can learn from the huge amount of open data that competes with, for example, "Amazon Alexa" and "Apple Siri", then you have given yourself an edge that you have always been search.

www.ingramcontent.com/pod-product-compliance
Lightning Source LLC
Chambersburg PA
CBHW022157150726
47992CB00002B/826